A Nelson Intensive English Course

COMPACT

Early Intermediate

Student's and Practice Book

Debra Powell *and*
Madeline McHugh

Contents and Map of the Book

SS = Student's Section   PS = Practice Section
GR = Grammar Reference   TS = Tapescripts

Many tongues

José
Spain

Ahmed   Angela   Miguel
Morocco   Switzerland   Colombia

Helen
Hong Kong

① *Saying what you think*

a These young people are students in London.

Who do you think speaks Arabic, Chinese, English, French, Italian, Spanish? In which countries do people speak these languages?

b Ask and answer in pairs:

Where	does	Helen Ahmed	come from?
Which languages	do	you they	speak (in Hong Kong . . .)?

vocabulary /vəˈkæbjəˌləri/, **vocabularies. 1** Some- N COUNT/
one's **vocabulary** is the total number of words in a UNCOUNT
language that he or she knows. EG *By the age of five,
the child has a working vocabulary of more than 2,000
words...* **2** The **vocabulary** of a language is the total N SING
number of words in it.   ⌂ lexicon

language /ˈlæŋgwɪdʒ/, **languages. 1** A **language** is **1.1** a
system of communication which consists of a set of N COUNT
sounds and written symbols which are used by the = tongue
people of a particular country or region for talking or
writing in. EG *...the history of the English language...
...a foreign language... I can speak six languages...*

② *First languages*

🔊 a **Listen to Helen, Miguel and Ahmed talking.**

   1 Which of the speakers is a) bilingual (speaks two languages) b) multi-lingual (speaks more than two languages)?

   2 What do the speakers say about a) the languages they speak/read/write b) their mother tongue/first language?

b **Are there many people in your country/class who are bilingual/multi-lingual?**

③ *Using a dictionary*

a Look at the dictionary definitions of *language* and *vocabulary*. Then ask and answer the questions about *language* in pairs.

   1 How do you pronounce this word?

   2 Next to *language* is the letter N. What do you think it stands for?

   3 What does *language* mean?

   4 Which word means the same as *language*?

   5 How do you spell the plural of *language*?

b In pairs, ask and answer similar questions about *vocabulary*.

④ *Personal information*

🔊 a Listen to Angela and José talking to their English teacher. Write down their initials, family name, age, place of birth, nationality, their first language and other languages they speak.

b Now do the same for yourself. Then, in pairs, prepare the questions you will need to ask to find out about your partner (*example*: Where were you born?) and tell the class about him/her.

Example This is (name). His/Her family name is . . . etc.

日本語 Dansk

中文 தமிழ்

العربية العربية English

Español Ελληνικά

Русский язык

5 Languages people speak

a Do you know what languages these are? Can you guess the three most common languages in the world?

b Discuss the answers to the following questions in pairs. Then listen to the radio report and check your answers.

1 How many people speak English today?
2 Which people are the best linguists in the world?
3 Are many schoolchildren in London bilingual?
4 How many words are there in the English language?
5 How many people spoke English 2,000 years ago?

6 Language focus

do and *does*.

a Which sentence takes *do*? Which takes *does*?

1 Where _____ you come from?
2 My father _____ not speak English fluently.

What kind of sentences take *do* and *does*?

Now make sentences from these prompts.

Example language/you speak/home? = Which language do you speak at home?

3 where/your family live?

4 how/spell your name?
5 language/people in your country speak?
6 my grandmother/not speak Spanish/speak Basque.
7 Angela's father/not come from Switzerland/come from Italy.

b Write questions for these answers.

1 It means: 'able to speak two languages'.
2 It stands for *noun*.
3 No, he doesn't, but he understands it a little.
4 V-O-C-A-B-U-L-A-R-Y.

7 The good language learner

a In pairs, discuss what you think makes a good language learner.

b Now read these results of a language study and compare them with your ideas:

A good language learner is someone who:

1) enjoys communicating with others   2) is not afraid of making mistakes   3) is good at guessing
4) practises a lot   5) studies the grammar of the language   6) compares what he/she says to what native speakers say

c Are you/Is your partner a good language learner? Why?

8 Turn of phrase

a This sentence has two meanings. Can you guess them?

We don't speak the same language.

b Read the sentences and then match the expressions in italics with the phrases (a–c).

1 I *gave him my word* that I would come.
2 Please don't *breathe a word* to anyone.
3 You *took the words right out of my mouth*.

a promised him
b said exactly what I wanted to say
c talk about this

A la carte

Maxim Chinese
153–5 Northfield
Ave, W13
☏ 081–567 1719

A large menu specialising in Peking cuisine is offered at this large restaurant, which seats about 100 and stays open late. Vegetarian meals are included in the choice, and there are some interesting set meals. Diners with limited experience of Chinese food can ask the helpful young Oriental staff for help in choosing their meals. Service is cheerful and willing.

Tuttons
11–2 Russell St.
WC2
☏ 071-836 4141

This large, bright brasserie next to Covent Garden Market serves everything from a cup of coffee to a full meal. Popular snacks such as chicken liver pâté appear on the menu, and there are some unusual British regional specialities. Vegetarian meals are also available. Alternatively, customers can choose to have a drink in the Spanish-style bar downstairs, where spicy snacks are also served. Service is by cheerful young waitresses.

The Stockpot
6 Basil St, SW3
☏ 071-589 6827

This cheap and cheerful restaurant is very popular at lunch-times with tourists, shoppers and local office workers. The menu has something for everyone; omelettes, pasta dishes, salads, roast beef -- and lots more. Few main dishes cost more than £2. To start, there is a short list of popular items like soups, pâté, and melon, and, to finish, good home-made sweets such as crumble and sponge puddings, costing well under £1. For quick, simple daytime eating at very moderate cost, the Stockpot is ideal.

① Saying what you think

In pairs, say which of these foods you eat or don't eat:

brains	raw fish
cheese	seaweed
dog	shellfish
horse	squid

Example

I eat . . . all the time.	So do I.
I've never tried . . .	Neither have I.
I ate . . . once, and it was delicious/awful.	

② Eating out

a Look at these texts. Are they from a newspaper, a letter, or a guidebook?

b Which of these is the writer trying to do? Choose one.

  – recommend and give information.
  – say that none of the restaurants is any good.
  – say that some of the restaurants are better than others.

c Which restaurants would you recommend to these people? Why?

  a someone in a hurry
  b someone who doesn't eat meat or fish
  c someone who doesn't have much money

  Which restaurant would you go to yourself?

③ Using a dictionary

a In pairs match the adjectives below with the kinds of food.

Example stale – *bread*
fresh, mouldy, raw, ripe, rotten, sour, stale
bread, cheese, milk, meat, fruit, eggs

Now say which foods you would/wouldn't like to eat.

b Look at this list of foods.

banana, cocoa, coconut, black coffee, cheese, lemon, potato crisps, sugar, vinegar

Make a chart with the headings *sweet, sour, salty* and *bitter*. Now decide which flavour goes with which food. Can you think of other foods to write under the headings?

2
1 cheeseburger with chips
1 beefburger with chips
1 large coke
1 small orange juice

1
2 cheeseburgers with chips
1 large coke
1 small orange juice

3
1 cheeseburger with chips
1 beefburger with chips
1 large coke
1 large orange juice

4 *What would you like?*

a Listen to these three conversations. Which one takes place:

1 in a fast food take-away?
2 in a pub?
3 in a restaurant?

b Look at these orders and listen again. Write down the number of the girls' order.

5 *Language focus*

offers and requests

a In which of the examples in A is the speaker: a) offering (to do) something b) asking for something?

A	B
1 Can I get you anything to eat?	a Yes, thanks. That would be nice.
2 Can I have a menu, please?	b Yes, thank you. I'd love some more.
3 Can you pass the salt?	c No, thanks. I'm not hungry.
4 Would you bring me the bill, please?	d Here you are.
5 Would you like a cigarette?	e Yes, of course.
6 Could I get you some more coffee?	f No thank you. I don't smoke.

b Match the offers and requests in A with the replies in B. For some there is more than one correct reply.

MENU

£7.95

STARTERS
Prawn Cocktail
Egg Mayonnaise
Whitebait
Garlic Mushrooms

MAIN COURSE
Roast Beef
Grilled Plaice
Stuffed Chicken
Vegetable Lasagne

* * *

Selection of desserts

6 *Customer calls*

a Look at the menu and listen again to the conversation in the restaurant. Then, in pairs, take turns at being the waiter and the customer and make similar conversations, like this:

Are you ready to order?	I'd like . . .
Can / Could I get you anything to drink?	I'll have . . . Could I have . . . ?

b Now listen to the same customer. What does she complain about? What does the waiter offer to do? Make similar conversations in pairs using these prompts:

– milk/sour
– meal/cold
– meat/overcooked

7 *Turn of phrase*

a What do these expressions mean?

1 I could eat a horse.
2 He drinks like a fish.
3 He wolfed his meal down.

b What sayings about food are there in your language?

3 Strange but true

1 Saying what you think

a Match these superstitions with the pictures. In pairs, discuss whether they bring good or bad luck.

Walking under a ladder, touching wood, crossing your fingers, a horseshoe, breaking a mirror, Friday 13th

b What things are lucky or unlucky in your country? Do you believe in these superstitions? Why?/Why not?

2 Strange events

a In pairs, match the pictures with the descriptions.

1 Mr R K Wilson took this photograph in April 1934. He was driving by the side of Loch Ness in Scotland, when he saw a monster in the loch. He said the creature's neck was about 180 cm long.

2 In the early 1960s, a vicar took this photograph of the inside of his church in the North of England. When he was taking the photograph he did not see anything unusual. But when the film was developed, he noticed this strange figure in the corner.

3 In England, in March 1966, a fifteen-year-old boy took this photograph. He was walking back home from the shops, when he saw a strange orange-coloured light in the sky. It did not look like a star and the light was coming closer and closer. He ran home to get his camera.

Which of these stories is about a) visitors from another planet, b) monsters, c) ghosts?

b Imagine you are Mr Wilson/the vicar/the boy. Close your books and retell the stories to your partner. Do you know any similar stories?

3 I don't believe it!

a Listen to three people talking about the stories in exercise 2. Which story is each one talking about?

b Look at these opinions and then listen again. Which person says which opinion?

1 I suppose it could be true.
2 Some people believe anything, don't they?
3 Oh, yes. They definitely exist.
4 There could be some truth in it.
5 When we have some real proof, then I'll believe it.
6 I think it's a load of rubbish myself.

c In pairs, make a table with the headings *belief*, *disbelief* and *uncertainty* and put the opinions under the headings.

4 Language focus

past simple and past continuous

a **Look at these two sentences.**

1 Mr Wilson was driving by the side of the loch when he saw the monster.
2 The boy was walking home when he saw a strange orange light in the sky.

In sentence 1, *was driving* is the past continuous and *saw* is the past simple. Can you now find the same two forms in sentence 2?

b **Look at these two questions. Which one uses the past continuous and which one uses the past simple?**

3 What was the boy doing when he saw . . .
4 What did the boy do when he saw the . . .

How is the meaning of 3 different from 4? Now answer the questions.

c **Complete the story with the verbs below.**

be   drop   feel   hear   rain   see   shout   turn
walk

It was midnight. I _____ slowly down the street. It was cloudy and it _____ a little. I _____ very tired. Suddenly I _____ footsteps behind me. I _____ round, but there was no-one there. I continued walking more quickly. I _____ quite scared. I turned round again and _____ a man running towards me. 'Wait!' he _____. 'You _____ your purse at the bus stop.'

5 Horoscopes

In the Chinese horoscope, it is important which year you were born in. There is a special animal for every year. Look at this chart for people born between 1941 and 2000. Which animal are you?

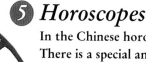

snake	intelligent and secretive
horse	charming and elegant
sheep	artistic and romantic
monkey	clever and good at languages
cock	honest and efficient
dog	kind and stubborn
pig	tolerant and popular
rat	sociable and hard-working
ox	independent and truthful
tiger	brave and quick-thinking
rabbit	polite and diplomatic
dragon	lucky and confident

Ask other people in the class questions about their horoscopes.
Example Which year were you born in? Do you think you are kind . . . ?

6 The Haunted House

Listen to these sounds and complete and continue this story. Use the past continuous and the past simple.

One night there was a strong wind and it _____ hard. I _____ along a country road that night, but the weather was so bad I decided to stop. I _____ to an old house and _____ the bell. An owl was hooting in the trees. I _____ footsteps and the door _____. Suddenly there _____ a horrible laugh and the sound of something dripping. Was it . . .?

7 Turn of phrase

Read the sentences on the left and then choose the best response for each one from the expressions on the right.

a Thank goodness I'll never see him again.

b I've got my driving test next week

c We lost the game by one point.

1 I'll keep my fingers crossed for you.
2 Touch wood.
3 Oh, bad luck!

That's entertainment

① *Saying what you think*

In groups, discuss which kinds of entertainment you like best.

- the cinema
- the theatre
- the opera
- the ballet

- concerts
- nightclubs
- discos
- jazz clubs

Dance

● **LE CORSAIRE**
The Kirov Ballet in the full-length Corsaire, in a production by Pyotr Gusev.

Theatre

● **BERNADETTE**
The miracle of Lourdes comes to the stage in this new musical by Gwyn and Maureen Hughes. With Natalie Wright.

● **SINGER**
A triumphant performance from Antony Sher in Peter Flannery's modern Jacobean tragi-comedy. Terry Hands directs.

Classical

● **BEETHOVEN'S MISSA SOLEMNIS**
Missa Solemnis comes from the London Oriana Choir and RPO conducted by Leon Lovett. Soloists are Sarah Leonard, Ameral Gunson, Neil Mackie and Alastair Miles.

Chopin Impromptus and Sonata No2 in Bb minor open Portuguese pianist Maria José Morais' recital; to continue with three Scarlatti sonatas, Ravel's Sonatina, two Rachmaninov preludes and Brahms' Paganini Variations.

Mozart's Requiem performed by the University of London Orchestra and Chorus, conductor Mark Shanahan; preceded by the 'Haffner' Symphony

Cinema

Cinema Electric
Fri at 11.00: **'Purple Rain'** (Albert Magnoli, 1984, US) Prince. + **'Under the Cherry Moon'** (Prince, 1986, US) Prince.
Sat at 11.00: **'Beetlejuice'** (Tim Burton, 1988, US) Michael Keaton. + **'Sir Henry at Rawlinson End'** (Steve Roberts, 1980, GB) Vivien Stanshall, Trevor Howard.

High Street Odeon
Fri, Sat at 11.15: **'Pretty Woman'** (11.25)
2. **'Look Who's Talking'** 3. **'The Krays'** (11.25)
4. **'The War of the Roses'** (11.25)

Jazz

● **CHRIS BARBER'S JAZZ & BLUES BAND**
Vaunted mainstay of the European tour circuits, cleverly re-interpreting mainstream styles with an obvious bias towards New Orleans.

RESTAURANT BAR
JAZZ AFRICAN LATIN

DOORS OPEN 7.30pm

THE COMEDY STORE

② *Going out or staying in?*

a Tell your partner how often you go out, and where you go, like this:

| I go to | the theatre ... | a lot. once or twice a month/year. from time to time. |
| I | hardly ever never | go to | the opera. ... |

b How often do you watch television or videos?

The average child in the United States watches 31 hours of television a week, and will see 26,000 murders before his/her eighteenth birthday.

Does this fact worry you? Why/Why not? Are you a TV addict?

③ *What's on?*

a This is part of the entertainments page of a London newspaper. Would you like to go to any of these events?

b Look at the words below. Which ones do you think have a positive meaning, and which ones have a negative meaning?

awful, boring, brilliant, dreadful, entertaining, excellent, fantastic, funny, great, magnificent

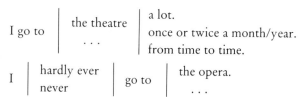 Listen to three visitors to London describing events they have seen. What events did each speaker enjoy/not enjoy?

c Listen again and find which speaker says:

1 go to a couple of concerts
2 leave on Monday
3 come back next year
4 take it easy for a few days
5 cash some more traveller's cheques

Then complete the first part of each sentence.

Example   *I'm going to* go to a couple of concerts.

4 Language focus

will* or *going to

a Look at this conversation.

– *Are you going to eat out* tonight?
– Yes, I think so.
– Have you tried 'Spaghetti Opera'?
– That's a good idea. *I'll phone* now and book a table.

**Which of the verbs in italics refers to something:
a) planned or thought about before b) decided at the time of speaking?**

Use these prompts to make similar conversations.

1 /you/go and see that new film?
   Yes, I think so.
   /bought the tickets?
   No. That's a good idea. I/get them now.

2 How/we/get to the concert?
   By taxi.

/booked one?
Oh no, I forgot. I/book one now.

b When we decide something at the time of speaking, we often use *I think I'll* . . .

Example
– What are you going to do this evening?
– *I think I'll* go to the pub with Claudia.

Use these prompts to make similar conversations.

3 What/do/tonight?
   /not know./think/watch TV.

4 Which film/see tomorrow night?
   /not know./think/go to that new Brazilian one.

5 When/go/the Spanish dance performance?
   /think/tickets for next Thursday.

5 Making plans

a In pairs, study the London entertainments guide in exercise 3. Discuss which events you would like to see and plan a three day visit for Thursday, Friday and Saturday.

b Work with another pair, ask about their plans and tell them about yours, like this:

– What are you going to do on . . .?
– In the afternoon we're going to . . .
– Are you going to . . .?

6 World favourites

In groups, discuss what kind of films, TV, and music you like and which are your favourite actors, musicians, etc.

I love . . .,	it's fantastic.
My favourite . . . is . . .,	he's/she's great.
I can't stand . . .,	they're dreadful.

Can your group agree on a favourite film, actor, TV programme, etc?

7 Turn of phrase

Match the expressions with the illustrations. Can you explain what they mean?

1 She's always blowing her own trumpet.
2 She doesn't like being in the limelight.
3 She's a real prima donna.

Home sweet home

1 *Saying what you think*

a Look at the photographs. Where would you like to live and why?

b Match each of the words below with one or more of the photographs. Can you find other words to describe the places?

boring, clean, country, horrible, interesting, lovely, noisy, polluted, quiet, town

Now match the opposites in the list.

Example noisy – quiet

SPACIOUS 2-bedroomed, unfurnished flats. £225 pcm.

MODERN 3-bedroom unfurnished country cottage. One year tenancy available. Regret no pets or children.

PROFESSIONAL person to share house. Town centre 5 minutes. All mod cons. CD. Video. Microwave. £50 pw.

LARGE room in comfortable house. Use of all facilities. Female. Non-smoker preferred. £50 a week inclusive.

MODERN detached 3-bedroom estate house to let. Fully furnished for 1 year. £350 per month inclusive.

2 *A place to let*

Find the right advertisement for each person or family.

Jane Wright – Nurse. Non-smoker. Would like to rent a room in a family home.

The Andersons – A student couple. Looking for a furnished house to rent for a year or so.

Andrew Langley – Teacher. Smoker. Wants to share a house but does not have a car.

Anne Wilson – Divorced woman with a child. Would prefer a flat.

3 *Have you ever lived abroad?*

a Listen to the conversation and answer these questions.

1 Has Phyllis ever lived abroad?
2 Where did she live over ten years ago?
3 Where does she live now?
4 Where would Phyllis prefer to live? Why?

b Now listen again and complete these sentences.

5 Phyllis lived in _____ for _____ years.
6 She returned to England _____ years ago.
7 Phyllis thinks that home is _____.

4 Language focus

past simple or present perfect

a Look at these examples:

1 I've lived in England for almost ten years now.
2 I lived in Australia for twelve years.

Which sentence refers only to the past?
Which sentence refers to the past and the present?

b **Put the verbs in the conversation into the correct form, past simple or present perfect.**

1 _____ you ever _____ abroad? (*live*)
Yes, I _____ in Australia for ten years. (*live*)

2 He _____ for the same company for ten years now. (*work*)
He _____ there when he left school, didn't he? (*start*)

been or gone

Look at these examples, and match each one with one of the meanings below.

1 He's gone to Italy.
2 He's been to Italy.

a He's back here. He has come back from Italy.
b He's not here. He hasn't come back from Italy yet.

5 Where's home?

a Talk about the place where you live. Do you like living there? Why? Has it always been your home?

b Read the text. Where do the writer and her family live now?
Match the members of the writer's family with the places they call 'home':

England, Africa, Jamaica

Read the text again. Who has these feelings about home?

Home is the place where . . .

1 you can support your family easily.
2 you have always lived.
3 your family's history began.
4 you spent your childhood.

Which phrases and sentences give you the answers?

c Which person do you agree with? Why?
Where is 'home' for the writer? What do you think?

> *Where do I really belong? 'Home' my mother says, is in Jamaica, where she was born and grew up. But my father says that 'home' is where we are now, where he can feed and clothe his family comfortably and send his children to decent schools. My brother, Carlton, says 'home' is in Africa, where our ancestors came from hundreds of years ago. My sisters say they are English. They were born here in London and they have never lived in another country, so 'home' is not a problem for them. I suppose they are all right, in a way, but how can I fit all this together?*

6 Homes and holidays

In pairs, talk about the places you have lived in and the places you have been to. Ask your partner questions and find out:

– where his/her home is. (Where's your . . .?)
– how long he/she has lived there. (How long . . .?)
– if he/she has ever lived in/been to another country. (Have you ever . . .?)
– when and for how long. (When/How long did you . . .?)

When you have finished, tell the class about your partner.

7 Turn of phrase

a What do these expressions mean? Choose one and tell the class what you think.

1 A man's home is his castle.
2 Make yourself at home.
3 Home is where the heart is.

b What expressions or sayings about 'home' are there in your language?

The fairer sex?

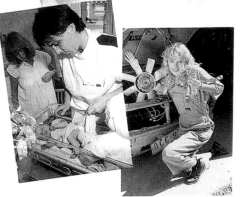

1 Saying what you think

a In groups, discuss who in your family is/was responsible for:

cleaning the house	raising the children
cooking meals	doing the gardening
general repairs	washing the car
mending clothes	shopping for food
earning money	doing the washing and ironing

Now tell the class what your group discussed.

b Do you think men and women in your family share jobs in the house equally?

2 Women's work?

a In pairs, say which of these jobs you think are traditional career choices for women and which are traditional choices for men.

car mechanic, electrician, engineer, housekeeper, lorry driver, nanny, nurse, office clerk, plumber, secretary

b Listen to the careers officer talking on the radio about career choices for women.

Does she say that they are a) not changing, b) becoming more traditional, or c) becoming less traditional?

Now answer these questions:

1 The careers officer gives two reasons why people's attitudes are changing. What are they?
2 What non-traditional career choice(s) does she mention for women/for men?
3 Does she believe that people's attitudes are changing? Do you agree with her?

c List three jobs you are considering now or considered when you were younger.

3 Using a dictionary

a Which of these words would you use to describe men, women or both men and women?

attractive, beautiful, clean-cut, good-looking, handsome, lovely, plain, pretty, ugly

b These words describe a person's character. Do you think the qualities they describe are positive or negative? Can any be both negative and positive?

1 aggressive   2 ambitious   3 bossy   4 conceited
5 confident   6 considerate   7 generous   8 kind
9 selfish

c Now write four or five sentences describing people you know.

Example My sister is attractive and confident, but she is also bossy.

The safer sex

The suggestion that women drivers have fewer accidents than men is perfectly believable. Women are not as aggressive as men, on and off the road, and, as a long-distance lorry driver, I feel that women are also far more considerate and much safer drivers than men.

Charlie Hicks, Borrowdale, Cumbria

4 Women drivers

a Read this short letter which appeared in a newspaper. What is the writer's job?

b Do you agree with the writer when he says that women drivers are safer, more considerate and less aggressive than men?

5 Language focus

adjectives in comparisons

a The comparative form is used to compare people, places or things. With a) one-syllable adjectives and b) two-syllable adjectives ending in 'y', the comparative form ends in a) -er, b) -ier. The comparative of other adjectives is formed with *more* or *less* (+ *adjective*). Some irregular comparatives: *good – better, bad – worse.*

Women drivers are	safer	than men drivers.
	less safe	

Men drivers are	more	aggressive than women drivers.
	less	

With short or long adjectives, *(not) as + adjective + as* can also be used.

Men drivers are not as considerate as women drivers.

b What is the comparative form of these adjectives? Think of some others.

ambitious, bad, bossy, conceited, considerate, good, kind, ugly

c Now write statements of your own comparing men and women. Use the words in exercise 3 and any other words for describing people that you know.

6 Women at work

a Before you read the text, say whether you think these statements about women in Britain are true or false.

1 80% of girls stop studying physics at the age of thirteen.
2 Over half of all qualified doctors are women.
3 Very few women become branch managers of banks.
4 Only 22% of men and women share the housework equally.

Now read the article to see if your guesses were correct.

b Read the text again. Which of the words or phrases in italics are similar in meaning to:

1 given a more important job   5 type (verb)
2 free from tradition   6 get dirty
3 to be paid as much as men   7 employers
4 belief that men are better than women

Why does the writer say that 'today's woman is not as liberated as she says she is'?

c Do the majority of women in your country still choose traditional jobs? Is this changing?

A new report reveals that today's woman isn't as *liberated* as she says she is. Women may demand sexual equality and *equal pay*, but in reality, it seems, the majority still prefer to *tap away at keyboards* than *get their fingers greasy* under the bonnet of a car. But it's not all the women's fault. The attitude of male *bosses* is also to blame. Women who apply for jobs that are traditionally 'men's jobs' are less likely to be *promoted*. And those that get promoted have to wait longer for it to happen.

The report also says that:
1) Despite a national shortage of mathematics and physics teachers, 80% of girls opt out of physics at the age of thirteen.
2) Though nearly half of all newly qualified doctors are women, most of the top jobs go to men. 3) In banking, where there are more women than men, only a handful of women get to be branch managers – 5% at Lloyds and 8% at Barclays. But *male chauvinism* begins at home. Only 22% of men and women admit they share domestic chores equally.

7 Turn of phrase

a Read the beginning of this well-known English expression. In pairs, suggest an ending for it.

A woman's work . . .

b What sayings are there about men and women in your language?

Life is for living

1 Saying what you think

a **Match the magazines with these hobbies:**

body-building, coin collecting, computer games, dance, knitting, photography.

b **Ask your partner if he/she is interested in any of the above. Have you got any different hobbies?**

2 The great outdoors

a **Listen to these people talking about the three hobbies below. Which hobby is each one talking about?**

cascade climbing, hang-gliding, wild camping

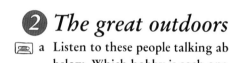

b **Which speaker says these phrases?**

1 It's like dreaming that you're flying.
2 I really enjoy relaxing, eating and sleeping.
3 I wanted to do something different.
4 I loved waking up in the early hours of the morning.
5 I was quite scared of doing it myself.
6 I'd like to go to Canada.

Listen again and check your answers.

3 Dull or exciting?

a **In groups, match these adjectives with different hobbies.**

challenging, dangerous, difficult, dull, exciting, expensive, healthy, relaxing, time-consuming.

b **In groups, talk about which new hobbies you would or would not like to try.**

I'd like to try	I think it's probably very
I don't really fancy	I think it's too

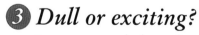

How about you? What would you (not) like to try?

4 Language focus

to and -ing

a Look at these examples.

1 I like learning foreign languages.
2 I would like to learn a foreign language.

Learning is a gerund, *to learn* is an infinitive.

Verbs usually followed by the gerund: *like, enjoy, love, hate, fancy, suggest*; and by the infinitive: *would like, want, need, decide, intend.*

Make sentences about hobbies, using some of these verbs with the gerund or infinitive.

Example I enjoy cooking. I'd like to know about Japanese food.

The gerund is also used after some phrases: *interested in, scared of, feel like, can't stand, keen on, good at*

b Complete this paragraph with the verbs in the list. Put them into the correct form: the gerund or the infinitive.

be, become, go, join, run, stop, train

When I was younger, I wanted _____ a professional athlete. I was very good at _____ when I was at school, and one of my friends suggested _____ a local athletics club. At first I was very keen on _____ as often as possible, but after a few months, it became too time-consuming. Sometimes I didn't feel like _____ out in the cold and rain and I decided _____ training every day. Now I suppose running is my hobby, but I'm not interested in _____ a professional any more.

5 Life begins at sixty

a What do you think are the usual hobbies and interests of a sixty-year-old grandmother? Tell the class.

Read the text quickly and find out what this grandmother is interested in, and what she intends to do next year.

Sixty-year-old grandmother, Fiona McFee, is going to retire next year and she has decided to realise a childhood dream and sail around the coast of Scotland in a small boat. Although the inside of the cabin is very cosy it has no running water or electricity. Fiona says she can live without these mod cons but she intends to take her portable CD player, her hot water bottle and a stack of books to make sure life isn't too uncomfortable.

We asked her if she was scared of being at sea for so long. She said, "Well, I'm going to take plenty of maps and a good compass. Anyway I'm not afraid of drowning because I love the sea – I just hope it loves me. Fiona certainly has plenty of energy; in her spare time, she enjoys playing the clarinet, rock-climbing, canoeing and tap-dancing. Although she is sixty, she doesn't want to have a quiet and peaceful life. "I'm looking forward to having fun in retirement and that's exactly why I'd like to be a sailor for a while."

b In pairs, find words or phrases in the text which mean:

1 the time when you are a child
2 where the land meets the sea
3 warm and comfortable
4 afraid
5 a lot of
6 death by water

c In pairs, find the verbs and phrases which are followed by gerunds or infinitives.

6 Turn of phrase

a One of the world's favourite pastimes is playing cards. Which games do you know? Tell the class.

b Which of the sayings (a–c) would you use to describe these types of people (1–3)?

1 Someone who does not give all of her information at once.
2 Someone who doesn't show what she is feeling.
3 Someone who is open and honest.

a She's poker-faced.
b She puts all her cards on the table.
c She keeps a few cards up her sleeve.

8

Changing style

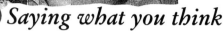

A

1 Saying what you think

Do you like any of the fashions in the photographs? What kind of clothes do you like? In pairs, discuss what you usually wear for work, for parties and at the weekend.

B **C**

2 How we used to look

a In pairs, decide whether each photograph was taken in the 1950s, 1960s, early 1970s or the late 1970s/early 1980s.

Now match these descriptions of clothes and hairstyles with the pictures.

1 Long skirts and dresses
  flared trousers
  necklaces and bracelets
  very long hair

2 metal chains
  leather jackets
  dyed spiky hair
  very tight trousers

3 T-shirts
  full skirts
  jeans
  pony tails or short greased hair

4 dark sunglasses
  mini skirts
  black eye make-up
  straight hair with a fringe

D

b Listen to the fashion editor of a magazine talking about past fashions. Check your answers to part a.

c In pairs discuss what you/your parents/your grandparents used to wear.

In my grandparents' day, people used to wear . . .
What did your parents use to wear?

3 Language focus

used to

a Look at these phrases from the interview.

. . . it used to be very fashionable . . .
. . . men didn't use to have long hair.

Does *used to* . . . mean:

1 something in the past which is the same today?
2 something in the past which is different from today?

b Study this chart to see how to make statements comparing the past with the present.

In the last century,			used to . . .		today
In the old days,	people		didn't use	but	nowadays
A long time ago,			to . . .		these days

Write sentences using the table and prompts.

Example women/have lots of children/have smaller families.

  In the last century, women used to have lots of children but today they have smaller families.

1 people/write by hand/use typewriters and computers.
2 all women/wear long dresses/wear all kinds of clothes.
3 people/listen to the radio/many people watch TV.
4 people/(not) travel very much/lots of people travel.
5 fashion/(not) change so quickly/it changes often.

I didn't use to look like this; I created my own image. When I was a girl, I used to look like _____. I enjoyed school. I used to be one of the best students at school. But I hated sitting still. You know, I could eat like a horse but I never got fat because I _____. I was very good at sport, too. When I was at school in Jamaica I wanted to become a _____ but then in my early teens we moved to New York. I was the only black girl in the school and I used to feel _____. But it was there I learned about Theatre and

Drama and that's when I became interested in _____. I suppose it was then, in my late teens, that I began to change my image. When I was 13 or 14, people used to think _____, now everybody thinks I'm 17 – I must be getting younger.

4 I used to be different

a Work in pairs. Student A: read the text about Grace Jones on this page. Ask and answer questions with your partner to find the missing information. Student B: turn to the text on page 48.

b Write down the questions you asked to find the missing information.

Example What did she use to look like when she was a girl?

5 Using a dictionary

a In groups, look up the dictionary definitions of these words and then put them under the headings *style*, *colour*, *material* and *item*.

Example colour – beige   *style* – baggy

baggy, beige, black, cotton, denim, dress, fitted, full, greenish, jacket, jeans, leather, long, purple, shirt, short, skirt, sleeveless, straight, suede, sweater, tight, top, trousers, turquoise, woollen.

b The table shows the order of adjectives before items of clothing. Using the vocabulary in part a, make examples of clothes that you would or wouldn't like to wear.

would like to wear	wouldn't like to wear
a pair of tight black leather trousers	a sleeveless woollen sweater

6 Biography

a The personal details of pop singer, **Yazz**, are incomplete and have been put beside the wrong headings. Put the information with the correct heading. Then listen to the radio DJ to complete the information.

Job	_____ May 19 _____
Real name	Father from _____, mother from_____
Date of birth	Fashion model in _____
Previous job	Yasmin Evans
Interests	Singer
Diet	Italy _____
Family	Macrobiotic – _____, _____ and seaweed, no _____ or dairy produce
Favourite country	Sport, _____ fit

b In pairs, use these notes to write the biography of Yazz like this:

Yazz is a . . . She was born on . . . and her real name is . . . She used to . . .

c In groups, prepare a short biography of another famous person. Tell the class the details and let them guess who it is.

7 Turn of phrase

Complete the sayings with these items of clothing.

shoes, belts, trousers

a His wife *wears the* _____ in that house.
b I wouldn't like to *be in her* _____.
c We all have to *tighten our* _____.

Can you explain the meanings of the sayings?

Facts and figures

1 Saying what you think

a Look at the animal in the photograph. Do you think it is ugly or attractive?

b Are there any animals you really like, dislike or are afraid of? Tell the class what these animals are and how you feel about them, like this:

I think . . . are really frightening.
I'm scared of . . .
I like/love/can't stand . . .

2 The poison-arrow frog

Before you listen to this interview, make sure that you know the meaning of these words:

arrow, tropical, stream, forest, treetop

a Listen to the first half of the interview and find out how:

1 Jayne Gray became interested in frogs.
2 the poison-arrow frog got its name.

b Now listen to the second half of the interview and write down some facts about the frog's size, appearance and where it lives.

3 Cities

a Read the texts quickly and match them with the titles. There is one title too many.

The fastest-growing city   The oldest city   The largest town
The cheapest city   The longest name

b Read the texts again and mark these statements as true or false.

1 London is about the same size as Switzerland.
2 There are about 6.2 million people living in Switzerland.
3 Krung Thep and Bangkok are the same place.
4 The Dutchman paid the Indians $24 for Manhattan.
5 New York used to be called New Amsterdam.

c Which city in your country is the oldest/cheapest to live in? Which is the most crowded?

1 Mount Isa, a town in Queensland, Australia, spreads over almost 41,000 square kilometres. It covers an area 26 times greater than that of London and is about the same size as Switzerland.

2 Mexico City is at present growing at a rate of 25 percent every 5 years. With a population of 16 million it is estimated that by the year 2000, it will be over 31 million. This is 5 times as many people as there are in Switzerland at present.

3 Krung Thep is the shortened name of the capital of Thailand, known in the West as Bangkok. Its full name has 167 letters!

4 In 1626 a Dutchman bought an island in America from some local Indians. He gave them some cloth and beads worth about $24 for an area of land that covered 57 square kilometres (22 sq miles). It was a bargain. He had bought Manhattan, the most crowded and expensive island in the world. He named his town New Amsterdam but it was later renamed New York.

4 Language focus

superlative adjectives

The superlative form is used to compare more than two people, places or things. One-syllable adjectives and some two-syllable adjectives form the superlative with *adjective* + *-est*. With longer adjectives, it is formed with *most/least* + *adjective*. Some irregular superlatives: good – *best*, bad – *worst*.

Mount Isa is the largest town in the world. (It is larger than all the others.)
Manhattan is the most expensive island in the world to live in. (It is more expensive than all the others.)

Put the adjectives below into their comparative and superlative forms:

bad, crowded, expensive, far, good, heavy, hot, large, long, successful, tall, young

5 Do you know?

Complete the facts using the superlative form of some of the adjectives in the Language focus.

Example The longest underground in the world is the London Underground. It is 400 km (247 miles) long.

1 One of _____ films ever made was *Star Trek*. It cost $21 million to make.
2 _____ man in history was an American, Robert Wadlow. He was 272 cm tall (8 ft 11.1 inches) when he died.
3 The Beatles were _____ pop group of all time. They sold over 1 billion discs and tapes.
4 _____ woman ever recorded was Mrs Percy Pearl Washington. She weighed 399.1 kilograms (880 lb).
5 _____ place in the world is Death Valley, California, where one summer the temperature was over 120°F (48.9°C) for 43 days in a row.

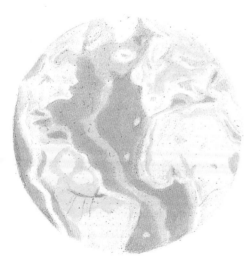

6 Quiz

In groups, see how many of these questions you can answer.

In the world, what is the:
1 longest river?
2 largest island?
3 highest waterfall?
4 deepest ocean?
5 largest desert?
6 smallest continent?
7 largest lake?

Which group got the most correct answers?

7 Turn of phrase

Say how you would finish this well-known expression:

A man's best friend is . . .

Now write your own expression beginning:

A woman's best friend is . . .

Take a break!

1 Saying what you think

a What's most important to you when you take a holiday? Choose the three most important things from the list. Tell the class, like this:

. . . is/are important to me because . . .

beautiful countryside, friendly people, good food, good weather, historic places, museums and art galleries, nice beaches, nightlife, shopping, sports facilities

b Where would you like to take your next holiday? Why?

WE LOVE YOU BRITISH

Britain has taken £6.2 billion from a record 15.4 million foreign tourists. Tourists put the charm of the British people as the most enjoyable part of their stay. The countryside and historic places are also remembered fondly. Britain has now become the world's fifth most popular holiday destination behind the United States, Italy, France and Spain.

British Tourist Association chief Michael Medicott said: 'The number of tourists coming to Britain has been increasing so that overall, this year should be as good as the last.' Estimates are that tourism will be worth more than £23 billion by 1994.

2 Best of Britain

a Read the article and find the answers to these questions:

1 What do tourists like about Britain?
2 Which country in the world is the most popular with tourists?
3 Have more or fewer tourists been coming to Britain in recent years?

b What do you think tourists like most about your country?

3 Language focus

present perfect simple and present perfect continuous

a The present perfect continuous is used to stress that an activity has continued from a time in the past until now. The present perfect simple is used for single or repeated actions.

1 I've *been taking* photos all day.
2 I've *taken* 20 photos of Westminster Abbey.

Which form is used in each sentence?

b Now go back to the article in exercise 2 and find examples of the present perfect simple and continuous.

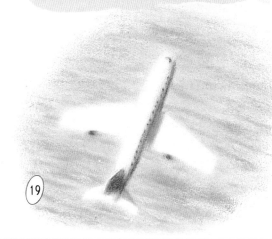

4 Visitors to London

a Look at the conversation between two people visiting London. Put the verbs in brackets in the present perfect simple or present perfect continuous.

A Hi. Sorry I'm late. _____ you _____ long? (*wait*)

B No, I _____ just _____ (*arrive*), actually. I _____ (*shop*) for presents. I think I _____ (*buy*) them all now.

A Good. Ugh! I suppose this must be typically English weather.

B I suppose so. It _____ (*rain*) all morning. Anyway, what about you? What _____ you _____ (*do*)?

A Me? I _____ (*write*) postcards all morning. I think I _____ (*write*) them all now.

B Good. Where shall we go now then?

A Let's see, we _____ (*seen*) St Paul's Cathedral, Westminster Abbey, Big Ben. We _____ (*not be*) to the Tower of London, yet.

B The Tower of London's fine with me. Oh look. There's a taxi!

b Now listen to the tape and check your answers.

Trans-Canada Camping/Train Adventure
Have fun travelling across the world's second largest country. You'll really get to know Canada. You will also enjoy the active nightlife of places like Vancouver and Montreal as well as the peace of a campfire in the wilderness.

Discover New York
Explore all the exciting places you've ever heard about – Wall Street, Times Square, Broadway – perhaps an exciting helicopter flight among the skyscrapers or a boat trip around Manhattan and the Statue of Liberty. Enjoy restaurants, galleries, museums, wonderful shopping and the hit shows on Broadway at night. Optional day tour of Niagara Falls.
Hawaii
In Exotic Honolulu, on the island of Oahu, you will find colourful Chinatown, many exciting shops and restaurants, and, of course, the world-famous Waikiki Beach. There are plenty of opportunities for sailing, surfing, golf and tennis.

5 The Tower of London

a What do you know about the Tower of London.

b Listen to a guide talking about the Tower of London and Traitors' Gate. Does the guide say (a) or (b)?

Part 1 The Tower of London:

1 was built in the a) *seventh* b) *eleventh* century.
2 Monarchs have used it as a) *a fortress* b) *a castle*,
3 a palace and a) *a gaol* b) *a prison*.
4 It was used as a palace by James a) *I* b) *IV*.
5 The Tower has always guarded the a) *Crown* b) *State* Jewels.

Part 2 Traitors' Gate:

6 was used as a) *an entrance to* b) *an exit from* the Tower.
7 Many famous a) *people* b) *prisoners* have passed through Traitors' Gate.

c Have you seen any other famous buildings? Tell the class what you thought of them.

6 Holiday plans

a Imagine that you have two weeks to take a holiday in either Canada or the United States. Look at the holiday advertisements and then, in groups, agree on a holiday you would all like to take.

b Tell the class which holiday your group is taking, and why you decided on that one. Which was the most popular holiday in the class?

7 Turn of phrase

Look at these expressions. Which ones would you say to someone who:

– is going away on a journey?
– has just come back from a journey?

Safe journey.   Welcome home.   Take care.   Have a good time.

Nobody's perfect

① Saying what you think

Have you ever tried to give up any of these things? Do you know anyone who has tried? Were you/they successful? Tell the class.

I	tried to give up . . .	but I couldn't.
	stopped . . .	but I went back to it.

I gave up . . . years ago.

② Breaking the habit

a You are going to hear a radio interview with Dr John Richards who is giving advice on giving up chocolate. Before you listen, make sure you know the meanings of these words:

cut down, addicted, addictive, chemicals

Listen to the first part of the tape and finish these statements.

1 A 'chocoholic' is someone who _____.
2 Chocolate contains chemicals which _____.

b Now listen to the rest of the tape. Put the pieces of advice for someone who wants to give up chocolate in the order that you hear them.

1 Set yourself a weekly plan.   4 Keep a diary.
2 Treat yourself.   5 Have fresh fruit available.
3 Cut down gradually.

STOP SMOKING OR I'LL BRING DOWN THE JET

A HOLIDAY jet pilot threatened to land and call the police after a woman refused to stop smoking.

He warned Maureen Harkavy: "Put that cigarette out or I'll land the plane and have you arrested."

Maureen, 47, was so shocked she wrote to the airline's chairman. But his reply was even ruder.

"You seem to think you have a God-given right to pollute your neighbours' atmosphere," wrote John Ferriday of Paramount Airways.

③ Fuming

a Read the first half of this article and then answer the questions.

1 What did Maureen Harkavy refuse to do?
2 What did the pilot threaten to do?
3 Who did Maureen write to?

The second half of the story has been jumbled up. Put parts 1–4 in the right order. Explain why you have chosen that order.

b The same or different? Which word doesn't belong?

rude, offensive, polite, arrogant

c Who do you think was in the right, Maureen Harkavy or the pilot? Give reasons for your answers.

(1) Said Maureen: "I only found out about it when I was checking in. I'm a nervous flyer so I lit a cigarette during the flight. A stewardess asked me to put it out but I said I intended to carry on as there was no rule against smoking in the flight contract." She was just finishing her cigarette when the pilot arrived.

(2) "I've never seen such an arrogant letter," she said. "I don't think I'll ever fly again."

But there was a funny side. Maureen explained: "We were offered cigarettes from the duty-free trolley!"

(3) Mr Ferriday went on: "Believe me, you haven't. Expecially when you travel on my planes."

Maureen and her husband Michael were moved to a Paramount flight just before they left Portugal. But they were not told of the company's no smoking policy.

(4) "He was loud and offensive," said Maureen. "He said if I lit another cigarette he would land the plane at Bordeaux and hand me to the French police."

Later, from her home in Mosely, Birmingham, Maureen wrote to the company and received the rude reply.

4 Language focus

who or which

a Look at these examples:

1 The pilot who spoke to Maureen was loud and offensive.
2 The letter which she received from the airline's chairman was even ruder.

Why is *who* used in the first example and *which* in the second?

b Read these sentences about Maureen's experience and complete the sentences with *who* or *which*.

1 Maureen Harkavy and her husband were moved to another flight when the flight _____ they were booked to take was cancelled.

2 However, the assistant _____ made the change didn't tell them about the airline's no-smoking policy.
3 The stewardess _____ asked Maureen to stop was more polite than the pilot.
4 But Maureen refused, saying there was no ban against smoking in the contract _____ she'd been given.
5 Maureen later complained to the chairman of the airline, but the reply _____ she received was so rude she says she may never fly again.

5 I'd rather you didn't

a Listen and put the sentences below in the order in which you hear them.

1 You don't mind if I smoke, do you?
2 Can I get you another one?
3 I'm afraid not, I've arranged to go to the theatre.
4 Do you mind if I sit down?
5 Actually, I'd rather you didn't.
6 No, thank you very much.
7 Are you free on Friday?

Which sentences are ways of saying 'no'?

b What is Jane's reply when her visitor asks if he can sit down? Can you finish her sentence?

6 Polite refusals

a In pairs ask these questions and refuse politely, using:

| I'm afraid I | haven't. | No, thank you. |
| | can't. | I'd rather you didn't. |

1 Would you like something to eat?
2 Would you like to go to the cinema tonight?
3 Excuse me. Do you have change for a pound?
4 Do you mind if I open the window?

b Practise similar situations in pairs.

Student A: Ask your partner:

– for permission to do something.
– if he/she would like to go somewhere with you.

Student B: Refuse politely.

7 Turn of phrase

Where might you see these phrases?

1 Smoking can damage your health.
2 Low alcohol content.
3 No additives.
4 Sugar-free.

22

The value of money

1 Saying what you think

Money means different things to different people. Is money important to you? Why/Why not?

2 Who says what?

a Look at the photographs. Who do you think says:

1 We measure success by the profits we make.
2 I don't worry about it. As long as I've got enough to eat, and to have a few drinks at night, that's it, I'm happy.
3 Until it's actually changed to something, like a machine or a car, it's just useless.

b Now listen to these people saying what money means to them and check your answers. Do you agree with any of them? Why/Why not?

Mrs Cooper, aged 55. Banker.

Mark, aged 19. Student.

Paul, aged 33. Gard

STUDENT WITH A £30,000 PLAN

At five he was collecting old newspapers to make money. And when he was 15 he signed his schoolmates up to start a babysitting circle.

Now 20, third-year Cambridge University student Peter Blackburn is managing director of a company with a £30,000 turnover. And he reckons it will show a profit of more than £15,000 by next summer.

He set up Peter Blackburn Ltd last year to bring out a brand new, colour term planner that now students all over the UK are using.

'I felt that most of the planners going around were pretty unimaginative,' he says. 'I believed I could do a better job and decided to have a go.'

Blackburn admits that he is putting far more effort into the business than his computer studies course at university. While fellow students are out with their friends, he keeps in touch with his business headquarters in Lancashire by mobile phone. Before he set up the company, he spent one holiday preparing a plan that would convince his bank to lend him money.

'Most students work hard for a good degree because they believe that will help them get a job to support themselves,' he says. 'I work hard at my company because that is what will support me next year, after I leave college.'

Friends reckon that Blackburn will make £1 million within 5 years.

He is not quite so confident, however. 'There's a lot to be done yet,' he says.

3 A business brain

a Look at the headline and photograph of the article. Write down three questions that you would like to ask about Peter Blackburn.

Now read the article. Were your questions answered?

b Put these facts about Peter into the correct order.

1 He spent his holiday preparing a plan.
2 He collected newspapers.
3 He set up his own company.
4 He asked the bank for money.
5 He set up a babysitting circle.

c Find the words in column A in the article. Then match each word or phrase in A with its meaning in B.

A		B
1 turnover	a	thinks
2 reckons	b	sure
3 have a go	c	value of goods and services a business has sold
4 keeps in touch	d	communicates
5 confident	e	try

d Do you think Peter is right to put more effort into his business than into his computer course? Should he spend less time working and more time with his friends? Why/Why not?

4 Language focus

revision of tenses

a The article in exercise 3 describes past, present and future events or situations in Peter's life. Re-read the article.

1 Find five verbs that refer to Peter's past. What tense are they in?
2 Find five verbs that refer to his present. What tense are they in?
3 Find three sentences about the future. What verb do they all have in common?

when, while, before, after

b Look at these examples:

When he was nineteen
While he was at university
│ Peter set up his own company.

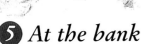

Before he finishes university, he will make a lot of money.
After he spent one holiday preparing a plan, he set up the company.

When, while, before and **after** can be used to:
– join two ideas.
– answer the question 'when'.

Example When did he set up his company?
　　　　While he was at university.

Now go back to the article and find examples of *when, while, before* and *after*.

c What other words or phrases to do with time can you find in the article?

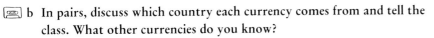

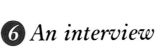

5 At the bank

a Look at this list of currencies and put them into the order in which you hear them on tape.

1 SFr 2 DM 3 ¥ 4 $ 5 £ 6 FFr 7 HK$ 8 Lit 9 Ptas

b In pairs, discuss which country each currency comes from and tell the class. What other currencies do you know?

6 An interview

a Look at your questions about Peter Blackburn from exercise 3. Ask your partner similar questions and any others to find out:

1 Why he/she decided to study English at your school.
2 What he/she does in his/her free time.
3 How he/she thinks learning English will help him/her in the future.

Make notes as you listen. When you have finished, tell the class about your partner.

b Use your notes from the interview to write a short paragraph about your partner.

7 Turn of phrase

Explain these sayings about money in your own words. Do you agree with them? Why/Why not?

1 Love of money is the root of all evil.
2 Money can't buy happiness.
3 Money doesn't grow on trees.

In the best of health

I Why weightlifting, Bev?

B Well, I felt very heavy and unfit after I'd had my first baby and I decided I wanted to get fit again. I'd seen a gym quite near my house, so one day I went in to join. This was about ten years ago and at that time not many women did body-building. In fact, they were very surprised to see a woman in there. At first the men didn't take me very seriously, but when I'd trained quite hard for a few weeks they began to realise I was really keen. Then they started to help me and give me advice and I improved a lot. You know, body-building changed my life, it gave me a lot more confidence.

I And, of course, now you are a big success.

B Yes, but body-building is a very time-consuming activity, but then I suppose I'm the kind of person who needs to do something one hundred percent or not at all.

1 Saying what you think

a Which of these do you do to stay healthy? Tell your partner.

- exercise regularly
- have a healthy diet
- get enough sleep
- take regular holidays

b Is your partner healthy? Which of the four ways to stay healthy do you think is most important? Why? Tell the class.

2 Superfit

a Read what Bev Hahn, champion body-builder, says about fitness, and, in pairs, put these sentences into the correct order.

1 She did not feel very fit.
2 The men realised she was very interested in body-building.
3 Bev Hahn had her first baby.
4 They helped her and gave her advice.
5 She joined a local gym.
6 She became a successful body-builder.

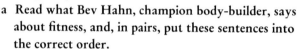

b Would you like to be as fit as Bev? Tell the class.

c Look at the picture and, in pairs, say the names of all the parts of the body which have numbers. Then write them down.

3 Language focus

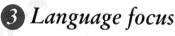

past perfect

a Look at these examples:

1 When I trained at the gym for a few weeks they helped me.
2 When I had trained at the gym for a few weeks they helped me.

Which sentence means a) they helped after the training b) they helped at the time of the training?

In pairs, read these sentences and say what they mean when you use (a) and when you use (b).

1 When I (a) *did* (b) *had done* body-building, I felt more confident.
2 My sister was very ill when she (a) *had* (b) *had had* her baby.
3 He stopped smoking when he (a) *was* (b) *had been* in hospital.
4 When I (a) *went* (b) *had been* on a fat-free diet, I felt much better.

b Rewrite the sentences using *after* instead of *when*.

c What does *'d* mean in *I'd had my first baby*? Why do you think it is written like this?

A   B

4 Six steps to health

Photo A shows how Sophie used to look.
And photo B shows how she looks now.

a Match the phrases on the left with the phrases on the
right to complete Sophie's six-point diet plan.

1 Throw out   a eating between meals.
2 Stop   b low-fat milk and cheese.
3 Change to   c new clothes – two sizes smaller.
4 Stop   d new hairstyle.
5 Get a   e all biscuits, cakes and chocolate.
6 Buy some   f drinking alcohol.

b In groups, write a six-point plan to improve your
health.

Example 1 Go to bed before midnight every night.

5 What's the matter?

a Listen to three short conversations. In each
conversation a) what's wrong b) what caused the
problem?

b Listen again and write down the sentences and
phrases for:

1 asking what the problem is
2 giving advice
3 giving sympathy/no sympathy
4 responding to advice

c In pairs, write down on a piece of paper two
examples of something wrong with someone and give
the reason.

Example You've got a swollen ankle because you fell
downstairs last night.

Give the paper to another pair of students. They
a) ask about the problem, b) explain the problem,
c) give sympathy/advice etc.

6 Food for thought

You will hear an interview with a doctor about a
strange disease called Kuru. The only people in the
world to suffer from this disease were the Fore Tribe
of Papua New Guinea – a tribe of cannibals.

a Listen to the first part of the interview and find out
what part of the body the tribe liked to eat and why,
and what the symptoms of Kuru were.

b Can you guess how the disease was passed on to
members of the tribe and why women got the disease
more often? Listen to the second part of the
interview to check your answers.

c What happened before:

1 the 1950s?
2 scientists discovered the cause of the disease?
3 the tribe stopped practising cannibalism?

What was the cure for Kuru?

7 Turn of phrase

Match the sayings on the left with the meanings on
the right.

1 She's a pain in the neck.
2 It's a real headache.
3 He sticks out like a sore
thumb.

a Someone/Something is
completely different
from everyone else.
b Someone/Something
annoys you.
c Someone/Something is
a problem.

Take care out there

Going out

The important thing is always to be aware and keep an eye open for possible problems. It's just a matter of common sense. Take sensible precautions: keep to routes which are well-lit and busy, avoid short-cuts through badly-lit, deserted areas, try to walk in the centre of the pavement at night, away from bushes and dark buildings.

If you think someone is following you on foot, cross the street, several times if necessary, and if you are still suspicious, walk to the busiest place you can find. Don't use cash dispensers late at night and don't carry lots of cash. Keep cheque cards and cash separate. If you are attacked, hand over your money – protect *yourself*. Attract attention if you can, but remember, *you* are more important.

1 Saying what you think

a What are the laws in your country regarding a) buying cigarettes and alcohol, b) dropping litter and c) making a noise?

b Do most people in your country obey these laws? Do you think they should? Tell the class.

2 Police advice

a Which three of these words and phrases are similar in meaning? Which one means the opposite?

against the law, illegal, legal, an offence

b Listen to a police officer giving advice to visitors to England. Put these topics into the order in which she talks about them.

noise, alcohol, smoking, traffic, litter

c Listen again and say whether these actions are illegal, or legal but not advisable.

1 buying alcohol if you are under 18 years old
2 making a noise at night
3 being careless when you cross the road
4 dropping litter in the street
5 buying cigarettes if you are under 16

Now make sentences from the above using *should not* or *must not.*

Example illegal You *must not* buy alcohol if you are under 18 years old.
not advisable You *shouldn't* make a noise at night.

3 Personal safety

a Is there much crime where you live? Do you go out alone at night, carry lots of cash or talk to strangers? What advice would you give to someone who was going out alone at night in an unsafe area? Make notes.

b Now read the text. Was your advice the same as in the text? Which words or phrases in the text mean:

1 look for
2 behaving in a sensible way
3 actions to stop something from happening
4 a shorter route than usual
5 think something is wrong
6 apart

c Why should you keep away from bushes and dark buildings? Why should you cross the street if you think someone is following you?

d Explain the meaning of the last two sentences of the text. Do you agree with them?

4 *Using a dictionary*

a **Look at these compound words from the text:**

common sense, badly-lit, well-lit, short-cut

Which are used in the text as nouns and which are used as adjectives?

b **Decide which of these adjectives can begin with *well-* and *short-*. Look them up in the dictionary to see if you were right. Finish the sentences with four of the words.**

built, fed, sighted, known, tempered

1 She wears glasses because she's very _____.
2 What does he look like? – He's tall and _____.
3 John's a _____ actor. Don't you recognise him?
4 The farm animals all looked healthy and _____.

5 *Language focus*

if or *when* in the zero conditional

a **Look at the examples below:**

1 *If* you think someone is following you, cross the street.
2 *When* you are at home, keep your doors locked.

What is the difference in meaning between *if* and *when* in the two examples? Which action is more likely to happen?

b **Which of the sentences below take *if*, and which take *when*?**

1 _____ someone tries to grab your bag, let go of it and scream.
2 _____ you answer the telephone, don't give your number.
3 Do not take any chances _____ you cross the road.
4 _____ you need any assistance, your local police will be pleased to help you.

6 *Giving advice*

In groups, write one or two paragraphs of advice for one of the following:

1 someone who finishes work late at night.
2 someone who is going to visit your country as a tourist.
3 someone who lives alone and is worried about his/her safety.

| Always . . . | You | must(n't) | . . . |
| Don't/Never . . . | | shouldn't | |

Avoid . . .   Be careful of . . .

Remember (not) to . . .   Try to . . .

When you have finished, read what you have written to the rest of the class.

7 *Turn of phrase*

a **Choose the sentence closest in meaning to *I could murder a steak*.**

I'm hungry   I like steak   I'd love a steak

b **Which one of the following can't you kill?**

time, money, sound, pain, a conversation.

The animal kingdom

1 Saying what you think

a Which animals can be used to make these products?

shoes, coats, cosmetics, jewellery, dog food

b Do you think it is right to use animals to make some/all of these things? Why/Why not?

2 The blue whale

a Whales are used to make some of these products. Do you know which ones?

soap, shoes, cameras, tennis rackets, violins, typewriters, earrings, golf balls, cat food, margarine, anti-freeze, photographic film

b Listen to the interview with a wildlife expert to find out which products are made from the whale. Write down the ones you hear.

Listen again and write down facts and figures about the blue whale's length, weight, average age, number of stomachs, and the amount of food it consumes per day. What other information about the blue whale did you hear?

c Do you think whale killing is necessary or not?

3 Animal or human?

a What do you think makes humans different from animals? Tell the class.

Read this text quickly and find out a) how many stories are told, and b) when the stories took place.

b Read the text again and in pairs say which word means:

1 to make a noise like a wolf.
2 to move on hands and feet.
3 a place for children who have no parents.
4 a group of wolves.
5 a large piece of ice.
6 very large.

c Now in pairs, retell the stories without looking at the book.

There are many stories about children who were brought up by wolves. The most famous is of two Indian girls, aged about seven and two years old. They were found in 1920 living with a pack of wolves. They crawled on all fours and howled like wolves. They were taken to an orphanage where they were taught to speak. The eldest learned to stand up and say a few words but she died when she was about 17 years old. Stories are also told about creatures who are half human and half animal. In 1957 in China, a young girl said that she was attacked by a strange hairy creature which walked on two legs. Later an apeman was found and killed by the local people. Its hands were preserved for everyone to see. The body of a similar creature was kept in a block of ice by an American circus performer. This apeman was two metres tall, also with huge hands. It was similar to Neanderthal man who lived about 50,000 years ago.

4 Language focus

the passive – present and past simple

a Look at these examples:

1 So many whales are killed each year.
2 Whale meat is given to our dogs and cats.
3 They were taken to an orphanage.
4 An apeman was found by the local people.

Find the verbs in each of the four sentences. They are all in the passive. Which verbs are in the present and which are in the past? Which verbs are singular and which are plural?

b Rewrite the sentences beginning:

1 Whale hunters . . .
2 People . . .
3 Some people . . .
4 The local people . . .

Why do you think it is better to write some sentences in the passive?

c Now look at the text in exercise 3 and write down all the verbs which are in the passive.

5 Are you an animal lover?

a Listen to two short conversations. In each conversation which of these topics are they discussing?

1 killing animals for their skins
2 bull-fighting
3 vegetarianism
4 using animals for scientific experiments
5 hunting as a sport
6 keeping animals as pets

b Listen again and write down the phrases they use to:

– introduce their opinion
– agree with someone
– disagree with someone

c In groups, discuss three of the topics in the list. Ask people for their opinions.

Example What do you think about . . .?
Do you agree with . . .?

Use some of the phrases you wrote down in part b to give your opinion, agree and disagree with others in the group. Does everyone agree? Tell the class.

6 Animals galore

a Match the animals with their group name.

Example a *pack* of wolves

wolves, cows, sheep, elephants, birds, dogs

flock, pack, herd

b Now can you match each animal with the noise it makes?

owl, cat, dog, lion, snake, frog

bark, roar, purr, hiss, hoot, croak

The sounds can describe the way people speak or laugh.

Example The teacher *roared* at the class.

Can you put the other sounds into sentences about people?

7 Turn of phrase

Finish the sentences on the left with the expressions on the right.

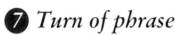

1 He'll always be the same, . . .
2 The party was great, . . .
3 I don't think I believe that, . . .

a . . . we had a whale of a time.
b . . . it sounds a bit fishy to me.
c . . . a leopard can't change its spots.

The business of sport

1 *Saying what you think*

a Which sports do you enjoy/hate doing and watching?

b Is there too much sport on the television/in the newspapers? Do people take it too seriously?

2 *A good match*

a With a partner, match the objects with some of the sports in the list.

boxing	fencing	American Football
golf	badminton	dog racing
skateboarding	cycling	motor racing
baseball	tennis	

 b Listen to these sounds of different sports. Match them with the rest of the sports in the list.

3 *Talking to a professional*

a Listen to this interview with Dave Oldham. He is eighteen years old and a professional sportsman. Which sport does he do?

b Listen again and mark these statements as true or false.

1 I've been doing the sport since I was twelve.
2 It took two years to reach a good standard.
3 I don't train every day.
4 It is becoming popular with girls.
5 I'm going to compete in Spain this year.
6 Youngsters will find it easy at the beginning.

④ Language focus

direct and indirect speech

a Which of these sentences is direct speech and which is indirect speech?

1 Dave said 'I've been doing the sport for three years.'
2 Dave said that he had been doing the sport for three years.

When sentences are changed from direct to indirect speech the verbs are usually changed like this:

do	did
did	did/had done
is doing	was doing
am going to do	was going to do
have done	had done
will do	would do

b The statements in exercise 3b are in direct speech. Correct the ones that are false and write all the statements in indirect speech.

⑤ World Cup drama

a Read the text to find the answers to these questions.

1 What are the two dramas described in the text?
2 Where do the incidents take place?

There is one example of direct speech in the text. Can you find it?

b Put the statements made by the following people or organisations into direct speech.

an official doctor,   a young woman arrested by the police,   Brazilian newspapers,   the Chilean players, FIFA

Example The Chilean players said 'Rojas is badly injured.'

5th September
A Brazilian airliner has crashed in the middle of the Amazon Jungle. Today a rescue party found 40 survivors. Brazilian newspapers said that the pilot had not heard air traffic control because he had switched radio stations to listen to the Brazil-Chile football match in Rio. The pilot's first question to the rescue party was, 'Who won?'
The answer was Brazil. But the match itself was a drama. In the 67th minute spectators said someone threw a rocket onto the pitch. The next minute, Roberto Rojas, the Chilean goalkeeper was on the ground in the middle of smoke and flames. All the Chilean players left the field. They said Rojas was badly injured, but later an official doctor checked Rojas and said that he could find no serious injury. Later the police arrested a young woman. She said she had thrown the rocket but she didn't realise it had hit the goalkeeper.
FIFA, the world football organisation, awarded the game to Brazil because, they said, Chile refused to continue the game.

⑥ Love it or hate it

a Listen to these five people talking about sport. Which of them:

1 is not interested in sport at all?
2 loves sport?
3 likes doing sport but isn't very good at it?
4 would like to do some sport again?
5 does some sport from time to time?

b Listen again and make notes on what the speakers say. Tell the class what they said.

c Now ask five different people how they feel about sport and write down their answers.

⑦ Turn of phrase

Who said what? Match these quotations with the pictures.

1 'I am the greatest.'
2 'I've never taken drugs in my life.'
3 'I drink 16 pints of lager a day. That's the only training I do.'

The happiest days of your life?

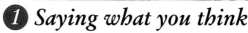

1 Saying what you think

Did you use to wear a school uniform at primary or secondary school? What was it like?

What are the advantages/disadvantages of wearing a uniform to school? Tell the class.

2 I hated school

a Listen to Chris talking about his experiences at boarding school. Find out if he enjoyed boarding school. Why/Why not?

b Listen again and in pairs write down as many things as you can about what he had to do and what he wasn't allowed to do.

c In what ways were/are your school experiences similar to, or different from Chris's? Tell your partner.

3 Language focus

have to, be allowed to

a Which of these sentences means something was
a) compulsory, b) not compulsory, c) forbidden?

1 The older boys didn't have to get special permission.
2 We weren't allowed to speak until the meal started.
3 We all had to get up at about half past seven.

b In pairs, use the table to make a list of three things you like/liked and three things you don't/didn't like about your school rules.

When I was at school	I we	was were had didn't have	(not) allowed	
At my school	I we	have don't have am are	(not) allowed	to . . .

Example We didn't have to do a lot of homework.
We had to do sport twice a week.

Now exchange your lists. Read your partner's list and tell the class what he/she liked/likes and disliked/dislikes about school.

c With your partner, write down six questions about school experiences.

Example Which languages did you have to study at secondary school?

Now ask two other people your questions and make a note of their answers. Then write a paragraph comparing the answers you have for each person.

Example Junko had to start school when she was six, but Maura had to start when she was four.

4 Small schools

a Read the text and find out what these words and phrases mean:

1 set up   3 state school   5 rent
2 dissatisfied with 4 curriculum   6 disused

What are the rules for setting up a new school in Denmark? Can you do the same thing in your country?

b Do you think the curriculum at Cooleenbridge School is good? Why/Why not? In groups decide on what you would include in a school curriculum for either 4–11 year olds or 12–18 year olds.

In Denmark, parents are allowed to set up a new school if they are dissatisfied with their local state school. Although these schools have to follow the national curriculum, they are allowed a lot of choice in deciding what to teach. Some of these new schools are called 'small schools' because the average number of pupils in them is only sixty, but a school has to have at least twenty-seven pupils.

Cooleenbridge School in Ireland, is a small school similar to the ones in Denmark. It was set up by parents who came from Holland, Germany, Czechoslovakia, England and other parts of Ireland. They came because they wanted to live in a rural area and to grow their own food. In June 1986, they decided to start a school. They rented an old, disused primary-school building and started with twenty-four children aged from four to twelve.

The teachers say, 'The important thing in school is doing, not sitting.' And so the curriculum includes yoga, baking, knitting, kite-making, pottery, music, fishing, drama and environmental river studies, as well as the more traditional reading, writing, maths and science.

5 Things we learn

a These are some of the things we can learn at school. They are in three categories.

Skills	*Knowledge*	*Experience*
reading and writing	learning about other	making friends
using a computer	countries	meeting different types of
	learning about the past	people

In groups put these different types of learning into one of the three categories and add some more examples.

typing,   speaking a foreign language,   understanding electricity, working in a group,   using a calculator,   playing a musical instrument, cooking,   learning about our health

b Write down your group's opinions on the following. Tell the class.

1 What are the three most important things to learn at school?
2 Are there exams for everything you learn at school? Why?/Why not?
3 What are the advantages and disadvantages of exams?

For Chinese schoolchildren learning to read and write is a difficult job. They have to know about 3,500 Chinese characters in order to read well. Here is a sentence in Chinese characters.

我 的 先 生 在 坐
my teacher is sitting

6 As easy as ABC

a In pairs, make some sentences out of these Chinese characters, then in groups, write a sentence in English. Each person then writes it into his/her own language.

b What do you think are the difficulties for children learning to read and write a) your language b) English?

7 Turn of phrase

Put these words into the correct sentences:

knowledge, know-all, know-how

1 He always thinks he knows more than everyone else – he's a real _____.
2 To the best of my _____ there are a lot of private schools in Japan.
3 You need a lot of technical _____ to operate these machines.

The 21st century

❶ Saying what you think

a What do you think life will be like in the next century? Tell the class.

Example
People will use solar energy to heat their homes.
Cars will be run on electricity.

b What other predictions can you make for the 21st century?

Living is easy

One thing's for sure, living will be much more convenient. Queuing up at the bank or supermarket will be a thing of the past – to order your new cheque book or do the weekly shopping you'll simply have to pick up the phone and key in your order. In fact, everything will be a lot more automated.

You probably won't have a robot to welcome you home from work with a nice cup of tea in ten years' time, but you'll certainly be able to phone home (from your mobile phone, of course) and tell the microwave and solar heating to switch themselves on. You may not have to leave home at all if you don't want to. Thanks to computers, many of us will have our office at home by the mid-1990s. Of course, we'll all know how to use computers by then. And the children won't even have to go to school. They'll probably study at home with a 'computer teacher' instead.

❷ Life in the future

a Read these predictions about life in ten years' time.

1 You'll do your shopping and banking by phone.
2 You probably won't own your own robot.
3 You may not have to leave home to go to work.
4 You'll only have to work two days a week.
5 Everyone will know how to use a computer.
6 Children will probably study at home with a computer teacher.

In pairs, say which predictions you agree with.

b Now read 'Living is easy'. Which of the predictions in (a) is not in the text?

Find words or phrases in the text that are similar in meaning to:

because of,   certain,   done by machines,   easier,   type in

c According to the text, people will probably spend a lot more time at home in ten years' time. Would you like to have your school or place of work at home? Why/Why not?

❸ Will anything stay the same?

 a Author Jeremy Lane makes predictions about changes that will take place in the next ten years. Listen to the conversation. Which two of these topics does he talk about?

1 the environment   3 work
2 holidays   4 health care

b Now listen to the conversation again. Which words or phrases in brackets best express what the speakers say?

1 Health care (*will/may*) improve.

2 Scientists (*will/may*) find a cure for cancer.
3 Scientists (*will/may*) invent vaccines for AIDS and the common cold.
4 People (*will probably/probably won't*) take 2 or 3 holidays a year.
5 Air fares (*will/will probably*) be cheaper.
6 People (*will/won't*) want to get a suntan.

c Mr Lane seems to think that life in the next century will be better than it is now. In groups, say whether you agree with him. Why/Why not?

4 Language focus

certainty and uncertainty

a In which of the examples below is the speaker/writer certain, and in which is he/she uncertain? Find the words or phrases that express uncertainty.

1 We will have more leisure time.
2 Scientists may/might find a cure for cancer.
3 We'll probably take three holidays a year.
4 People won't work a 40-hour week.

b Now go back to the article in exercise 2. Find the words and phrases which express certainty and uncertainty.

c Write three predictions for the next ten years. Show how certain you are about your predictions.

Example Men may fly to Jupiter in the next ten years.

5 Using a dictionary

a Look up the meanings of the words in A and then match them with the words in B.

Example word-processor

A	B
word	disc
solar	phone
compact	watch
mobile	energy
digital	processor

b Now match the words from part a with the pictures.

6 Survey

a In pairs, ask and answer these questions about your life in ten years' time.

Student A:

Will you use/have a mobile phone/personal computer/robot?

Do you think you will | work/study from home?
                       | take three holidays a year?

Will they find a cure for cancer/the common cold?

Student B:

Yes, I will./I (don't) think so./Yes, probably.
I don't know./Probably not./No, I won't.
No, definitely not.

b Now write some questions of your own and ask other people in the class.

7 Turn of phrase

a What does this saying mean? Do you agree with it? Do you have a similar expression in your own language?

Never put off until tomorrow what you can do today.

b What expressions about time (hours, days, future, past etc.) are there in your own language?

Wealth and poverty

❶ *Saying what you think*

a Look at these pictures. Where do you think the photographs were taken? Tell the class.

b In pairs, discuss which of these words and phrases best describe the people in the photographs.

low-paid, penniless, well-off, wealthy, rich, homeless, poor, down-and-out, unemployed

Which words are similar in meaning?

Text A Suresh

_____ year old Suresh comes from _____. His father is a _____ and his mother works at home. The family do not own any land and have no possessions except some _____ and _____. The family's total monthly income is _____. They live in a house made of _____ and _____ with a _____ roof. They cook with a _____ on the floor. The house has no _____ and no _____. If Suresh's family had more money they would _____ but they can't afford it now. Can you afford £5/£7/£12 a month? If you help us, one more child will learn to read and write, and one more family will have a better future.

❷ *Fighting poverty*

a In pairs, read the information about Suresh and Suhartono which comes from an aid agency called Plan International which works with children in developing countries. *Student A*: read Text A on this page. Ask Student B questions to complete the text. Then use the table to answer Student B's questions. *Student B*: turn to page 59.

Suhartono:

Age:	5	*Place of birth:* Indonesia
Father's job:	Peasant farmer	*Income:* £8.26 per month
Family house:	made of bamboo, mud floor, no water supply or toilet	
Possessions:	3 old wardrobes, 2 tables, 6 chairs, a bed, a radio, a bicycle, no land	

With more money: buy land and become an independent farmer

b How long could you live in your country on £8.26? In groups, list all the money you have spent in the last two days on:

food, drink, transport, clothes, entertainment, cigarettes

Which of these do you think are a) necessities b) luxuries? Would you spend less money on any of these things in order to give something to an aid agency?

❸ *Language focus*

if in the first and second conditional

a Look at these two examples:

1 If they had more money, they would send their child to school.

2 If you help us, one more child will learn to read and write.

Which sentence means:

a It is possible to change the situation.

b We do not know if the situation will change.

b Write sentences about what would be possible if Suresh's and Suhartono's situations were different.

Example If Suhartono's father earned more money, he would buy some land.

c Imagine you work for an aid agency. Write sentences to persuade people to give money.

Example If you send some money they will have a better future.

When Athina, the daughter of Christina Onassis was a baby she was given an island (cost unknown) by her family.

The Sultan of Brunei paid £25,000 to redecorate the ballroom of the London Grosvenor House Hotel for his son's 8th birthday party. The Sultan also paid world snooker champion, Steve Davis, £3,000 an hour to give his oldest son snooker lessons.

A British woman (name unknown) spent £25,000 on a present for her daughter, Julie. The present was a car number plate JUL 1E.

4 Expensive tastes

a What is the most expensive present you have ever a) **bought** b) **received**? There are some children in the world with very wealthy parents. Read these short articles to find out what some of these children have been given.

b In groups discuss what you would do if you had £3,000/£25,000/several million pounds to spend.

5 Using a dictionary

a The words *rich* and *poor* can have different meanings. Look up the dictionary definitions of the two words then finish these sentences using phrases with the words *rich* or *poor*.

Example Someone who cannot cook very well is a *poor cook*.

1 Someone who is often ill is in _____.
2 It is difficult to grow plants in _____.
3 _____ is food which is cooked in lots of oils and sauces.
4 Deep blues, reds and purples are very _____.
5 If you have _____ you probably wear glasses.

b **In pairs, make a list of all the things you can/can't do or have if you are rich or poor.**

Example If you are rich you can have lots of holidays. If you are poor you can't afford to buy a house.

6 The wealth in the world

a Which countries do you think are a) the richest b) the poorest in the world? Listen to this radio interview with an economist to see if you were right. Which of these countries is mentioned:

Afghanistan, Bermuda, Ethiopia, Pakistan, The United Arab Emirates, Australia, Britain, France, Paraguay, The United States of America, Bangladesh, Chad, India, Qatar

b **Listen again and answer these questions:**

1 What facts and figures does the economist give about:
– the average annual income of a) the richest b) the poorest countries in the world?
– the USA and India?
– Pakistan and Paraguay?
– 90% of the world's population?
– Britain?
2 Who is given as an example of a very wealthy man? How much money does he earn in an hour?

7 Turn of phrase

Match these expressions with their meaning.

1 She was *born with a silver spoon in her mouth*.
2 He's got *money to burn*!
3 She *hasn't got two pennies to rub together*.

a spends a lot of money on unnecessary things
b is from a rich family
c is poor

Hopes and plans

1 Saying what you think

What ambitions did you have when you were younger? Think about work, money, home, relationships, where you wanted to live.

Have you achieved them? Discuss in pairs and then tell the class.

Example
I wanted to be a footballer, but I became an engineer instead.

We want to earn £30,000 by 30 say teens

Youngsters want to be married with children and earning £30,000 a year by the time they are 30. But for many teenagers, their idea of having fun is staying at home and watching television, a survey reported yesterday.

Nursing and teaching were popular choices for the girls, while one in four boys wants to be a businessman or managers. But although the girls chose lower-paid jobs, both sexes said they hope to earn a salary of between £20,000 and £30,000. Two-thirds would like to be married by the time they are 30 and the quality they admire most in the opposite sex is good looks. Most boys prefer spending a quiet night watching TV with their girlfriend, but girls would rather go out to cinemas or discos.

Youngsters' favourite idea of home is a house in a small town, and cruelty to animals is the issue young people care about most, according to the survey by Barclays Bank.

2 Tycoon teens

a A group of British teenagers were asked about their ambitions. Read the report of the survey. Are their ambitions similar to your own? Discuss in pairs.

b Read the report again and write down the answer to these questions:

1 What characteristic do teenagers like the most in the opposite sex?
2 How do many of them like to spend their free time?
3 What problem worries them the most?
4 Who conducted the survey?

c Do you think the teenagers will achieve their ambitions? Why do you think the boys and girls chose different careers? Discuss in pairs and then tell the class what you decided.

3 Important issues

In the survey in exercise 2, the people were asked what they cared about. This is what they said.

cruelty to animals, education, famine, unemployment, nuclear war

In groups, put them in order of importance to you and add any other issues you care about. Tell the class and give your reasons.

4 *I'd really like to . . .*

a Listen to Richard and Nicole talking about their plans for the future. Which statements does Richard make and which statements does Nicole make? Two statements are not made by either of them.

1 I'm definitely going to go back to France.
2 I'd like to get a job with a design company.
3 I'll probably get married one day.
4 I'd like to travel some more.
5 I'd really like to learn Spanish.
6 I want to start my career and earn some money.
7 I want to have children one day.
8 I don't plan to move out just yet.
9 I'm going to do some courses in English.

b Listen again and answer these questions.

1 When did Richard leave school?
2 When does he start his course?
3 When is he going to try to get a job?
4 How long has Nicole been working as an au pair?
5 How much longer is she going to stay in England?
6 When is she going to go back to France?

5 *Language focus*

expressing hopes and plans for the future

a Look at these examples:

1 I'm *going to* do some courses in English.
2 I'd *like to* learn Spanish.

Which of the verbs in italics is similar in meaning to *want to* and which is similar in meaning to *plan to*?

b Use the table to help you write three statements about yourself

'm going to	be . . .	(next week/month)
plan to	have . . .	(by the time I am . . .)
want to	own . . .	(at the end of the month/year)
'd like to	go to . . .	

I

Example
I want to have my own home (by the time I'm 30).

would rather

a Look at this example from the text:

Girls *would rather* go out to cinemas or discos.

Would rather is a common way of stating preferences.

b In pairs ask and answer questions from the prompts like this:

learn English/Japanese

A Would you rather learn English or Japanese?
B I'd rather learn English.

1 study in Britain/your own country
2 stay at home this evening/go out
3 live in a city/the country

6 *Discussion*

In groups, tell one another about your hopes and plans for the future. Talk about work, home and family, travel, or money. Tell the class what the members of your group have said.

7 *Turn of phrase*

Match each of the expressions on the left with its meaning on the right.

1 You want the moon.
2 Look before you leap.
3 Don't let success go to your head.

a think before you act
b make you conceited
c want something you can't have

PRACTICE SECTION

1 a Read the text and find out what *official language* means.

Most countries have an official language. This is the language which is usually used in schools, in newspapers, on the television, etc. Often, people speak one language with their family and friends and use a different language at work or at school. For example, in Nigeria the official language is English but many people speak Ibo or Yoruba as their first language. Some countries have two official languages. For example, Wales has Welsh and English. Sometimes people cannot speak one of the official languages: a few people in Wales do not speak English.

The most common official language in the world is English, perhaps because it is spoken in the USA. When the United States became independent from Britain they voted which language to use: English or Dutch. They chose English – but only by one vote. Just think – you could be learning Dutch right now instead of English!

b Mark these statements as true or false. Correct the false statements.

1 People usually speak to their family in their first
  language.   T/F
2 Every country has one official language only.   T/F
3 Everyone in Britain can speak English.   T/F
4 Many countries in the world use English as their
  official language.   T/F

2 Read this information about Helen and then complete the questions below.

Example ...... name? Helen. – What's her first name?

First name	Helen	Place of birth	Hong Kong
Family name	Chan	Place of residence	London
Age	15	First language	Chinese
Nationality	British	Other languages	English

1 .... name?   Chan.
2 .... she?   Fifteen.
3 .... she?   British.
4 .... from?   Hong Kong.
5 .... live?   In London.
6 .... speak?   Chinese and
                                        English.
7 .... language? Chinese.

3 Read this description of Helen which uses the information in exercise 2. Then write a similar description of someone you know.

Helen Chan is fifteen years old. She is British. She was born in Hong Kong and now she lives in London with her parents. Her first language is Chinese, but she also speaks English fluently.

4 Look at this definition of the word *linguist*.

Someone who can speak several languages is a
l *inguist* ....

Now read these definitions and complete the words.

1 A book which has definitions of words is a
  d.................
2 If you speak a language very well you speak it
  f.................
3 If you speak two languages, you are b.................
4 The v................. of a language means the words in
  that language.
5 When you say every letter in a word, you
  s................. the word.
6 If you speak more than two languages very well, you
  are m.................

5 Correct this description of Miguel which contains grammar and spelling mistakes. G = grammar mistake, S = spelling mistake.

Miguel is born in Colombia but he came to	1G
Britain when he was two year old. His	1G
father speak English but his mother do not.	2G
She understand a little English but not	1G
much. Miguel is bilinguel. He say Spanish is	1S + 1G
his first linguage but now he speak English	1S + 1G
better. His parents does not speak English	1G
at home. Miguel a student at college. He	1G
wants to be a teacher.	

6 Revision spot

a Write these numbers in figures.

Example three hundred and seven = 307

1 five hundred and seventeen   ....
2 nine thousand and twelve   ....
3 thirty thousand   ....
4 two hundred and fifty thousand ....
5 eight million   ....

b Write these numbers in words

1 999 ....
2 1048 ....
3 36,000 ....
4 500,611 ....
5 6,000,000 ....

1 Match each statement with the correct reply.

1	I never eat squid.	a	So do I.
2	I've never tried brains.	b	Neither could I.
3	I eat cheese all the time.	c	So have I.
4	I couldn't eat dog.	d	Neither would I.
5	I've eaten seaweed a few times.	e	Neither have I.
6	I would never eat horse.	f	Neither do I.

2 a Write these words under the correct headings. Are there any kinds of food in this list that you don't eat in your own country?

apple   carrot   lamb   plaice   turkey
beef   cauliflower   melon   pork   veal
banana   chicken   mushroom   prawn   whitebait
cabbage   duck   pineapple   trout

Meat	Poultry	Fish/Seafood	Vegetables	Fruit

b What other words can you put under these headings?

3 Put the parts of this conversation in the right order.

a *I'll try the egg mayonnaise.*
b It's chicken stuffed with garlic and herb butter and rolled in breadcrumbs.
c *I'll have a beer.*
d Can I take your order, Sir?
e *That sounds nice. I'll have that.*
f Would you like anything to start with?
g *Yes, I think so. What's Chicken Kiev?*
h Chicken Kiev with egg mayonnaise to start. And can I get you anything to drink, sir?

4 Write what you would say in these situations.

a You have finished your meal. Ask the waiter to bring the bill.
Could you bring the bill, please?
b You need to borrow £5. Ask your friend.

....

c A friend has just arrived at your house. Offer her something to drink.

....

d A waiter has brought your soup but there is a hair in it. Complain.

....

e Your friend is out of cigarettes. Offer him one.

....

5 Revision spot

Write sentences about the picture using *there is /isn't* and *there are /aren't* and the words in the list.

Example There is some tea on the shelf.
    There isn't any milk.
    There are some . . .
    There aren't any . . .

bread   cheese   eggs   mouse   saucers
butter   coffee   flowers   newspapers   tea
cat   cups   fruit   plates
chairs   curtains   milk   saucepans

1 a Read this short story.

I was sitting at home one night last winter. I was watching a terrible programme on TV and I was feeling bored. I was thinking of going to bed when I heard a strange noise upstairs. There was no-one else in the house so I felt a little nervous. I switched off the TV and the lights in the living room and crept to the bottom of the stairs. I sat there silently for a few minutes. It was cold and I felt scared – I shivered. Then I heard it again. It was a noise like someone crying. I was so frightened I couldn't move. I stayed there for another twenty minutes.

Cover up the story and rewrite it from these prompts. Then check for mistakes.

I/at home/night/winter./a terrible programme/TV/ bored. I/going to bed/noise upstairs./no-one else/ house/I/nervous. I/TV and the lights/living-room and/ bottom of the stairs./there silently/minutes. It/cold and I/scared – I shivered. Then/again./noise like someone crying./so frightened I/move. I/there/twenty minutes.

b Write an ending for the story.

2 Read these definitions of types of people. Which word is each sentence defining? The first letter of the word is given.

Example A person who is not afraid of danger is
b.*rave*...........

1 Someone who does jobs quickly and well is
e..................

2 If you are friendly and enjoy meeting people, you
are s..................

3 If most people like you, you are p..................

4 A person who learns new things quickly and easily
is c..................

5 If you like making your own decisions, you are
i..................

6 Someone who tells the truth is h..................

7 A person who is caring and helpful is
k..................

8 People who never change their minds, even when
they are wrong, are s..................

9 A person who is good at drawing and painting is
a..................

10 A person who often wins things is l..................

3 These pictures show people experiencing bad luck. Write down what they were doing when suddenly something happened.

Example look/mirror/it/break
She was looking in the mirror, when suddenly it broke.

1 walk/ladder/stone/fall/head.   2 carry/pile of books/fall/stairs.

3 lie/bed/hear/strange noise outside.

4 Look back at the story in exercise 1. Write the questions to the answers.

1 .... ?
I was watching TV when I heard it.

2 .... ?
No, no-one else, only me.

3 .... ?
I switched off the TV and the lights in the living room.

4 .... ?
Well, then I crept to the bottom of the stairs.

5 .... ?
It sounded like someone crying.

6 .... ?
No, I was too frightened. I just stayed at the bottom of the stairs.

5 **Revision spot**

Complete the sentences with *do* or *does*.

1 My parents and I .... not speak English at home.

2 She .... not believe in ghosts, and neither .... I.

3 Some people .... not learn languages very quickly.

4 What .... 'confident' mean? .... you know?

5 The Loch Ness monster .... not appear very often.

6 .... this book have any ghost stories in it?

1 a This is part of an advertisement for the Edinburgh Festival. Read the text and find out a) when it takes place b) how you can find out more information.

The world's largest international arts festival takes place every August in Edinburgh, Scotland. For three weeks, artists and entertainers from all over the world meet in Scotland's capital city. There are actors, film directors, dancers, artists, and clowns. Some of them are very famous, some unknown.

This year we are going to have French opera, new films from Germany and Poland, writers from Japan, and an exciting new French circus called Archaos. This is a very different circus – they perform on motorbikes and lorries instead of on horses and elephants!

For details of all these events and many more, phone the Festival Office, Edinburgh 2264001.

b Now mark these statements as true or false. Correct the false statements.

1 The Festival is a festival of Scottish music.   T/F
2 It lasts for a month.   T/F
3 You can see films there.   T/F
4 All the performers and artists are European.   T/F
5 Archaos is a traditional French circus.   T/F

2 Read these descriptions of people and then the plans in the table below. Match the people and the plans. Then write about each person's plans.

1 Elsa is a student in her first year of a three-year cinematography course. Today is the last day of her holiday in the United States.
2 Philippe is a dance student in Paris. He will finish his course in two months. He loves modern dance and he plans to join a dance company in New York when he finishes his exams.
3 Jack and Amy are Americans visiting the Edinburgh Festival. They love the cinema and all kinds of entertainment. They want to see and do as much as possible in the next two weeks.

I am We are	going to	work in the USA. become a film director. see lots of films. study hard for the next two years. go to many events in the next two weeks. be a professional performer.

3 a Look at these future time phrases and prepositions. Write down some of your future plans.

Example
Tomorrow evening I'm going to stay at home and watch TV.
I'm going to get the theatre tickets at the weekend.

in	the morning/afternoon/evening; a couple of days/a few weeks etc.

on	Tuesday/Thursday etc; 20th August.	at	the weekend; seven o'clock etc.

this morning/afternoon/evening; tonight;
tomorrow afternoon/night etc;
next week/month/year.

4 Complete this conversation with the verbs in the list. Use *going to . . .* or *I'll . . .*

come, do, leave, see, stay

a – What .... you .... this evening?
b – I've got tickets for the cinema. I .... the new Swedish film. How about you?
c – Oh, I think I .... at home tonight.
d – Why don't you come with us?
e – What time .... you ....?
f – About seven.
g – OK. I .... with you. Thanks.

5 Write about three kinds of entertainment you never or hardly ever go to, and about three kinds you do go to, and explain why.

Example I never go to the ballet. I can't stand it.
I go to the cinema once or twice a week. I really enjoy it.

6 **Revision spot**

Complete this conversation with *can, could* or *would*. In some sentences it is possible to use two of the words.

a – .... you like to order now?
b – Yes, ... I have a tea, no sugar, please? What .... you like, Ann?
c – .... I have a black coffee, please?
d – Right. A tea and a black coffee. .... I get you anything else?
e – No thanks.

1 Choose the correct tense from the verbs in italics.

9,500 flee homes as forest fires spread

Forest fires are spreading rapidly, causing massive destruction, and thousands of families *left/have left*[1] their homes. Emergency services *began/have begun*[2] a major rescue operation, and are evacuating more than 9,500 people from remote areas in Canada.

The fires, many started by lightning, *spread/have spread*[3] quickly in the warm, dry winds which are still quite strong, and weathermen say more thunderstorms are on the way.

Last week, approximately 4,000 people in Manitoba *had/have had*[4] to be airlifted to safety. One fire-fighting helicopter *crashed/has crashed*[5] yesterday but the pilot *escaped/has escaped*[6] unhurt.

2 Complete the sentences. Put the verb in brackets in the past simple or present perfect.

1 .... you ever .... abroad? (*work*)

2 I .... never .... in a foreign country. (*live*)

3 He .... to France in 1976 and he .... never .... back to the UK since then. (*go/be*)

4 .... they ever .... in a foreign country before? (*live*)

5 I .... him in Madrid last week. (*meet*)

6 José! What a surprise to see you here in London! How long .... you .... here? (*be*)

3 What would you say in these situations? Use the words in brackets and *been* or *gone*.

1 Your friend is on holiday in Italy. He'll be back next week.

(*He/to Italy*) ....

2 Your friend has come back from Italy.

(*He/to Italy*) ....

3 You've just come back from your second trip to Spain.

(*I/to Spain/twice*) ....

4 You need to go out to post a letter. Leave a note for friend who will arrive while you are out.

(*I/to the post office. I'll be back soon.*) ....

4 Match words from the two columns to make different 'homes'. Then label the pictures.

block of	house
terraced	cottage
detached	flats
country	house
semi-detached	house

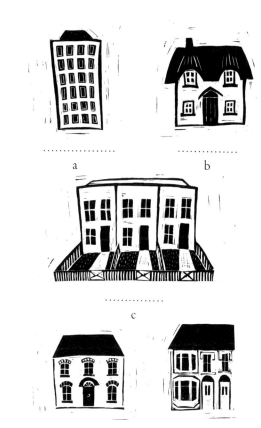

....
a   b

....
c

....
d   e

5 Match each of the words below with *house* or *home*. One word can go with both *house* and *home*.

.........boat, ...-grown, ...help, ...keeper, ...land, ...-made, ...owner, ...wife, ...work

Example *house*boat, *home*-grown.

6 Revision spot

Write *for* or *since* in the spaces provided.

1 I knew him .... many years.

2 I have lived here .... November.

3 I've known her .... we were children.

4 I've worked here .... five weeks.

5 I studied Italian .... many years.

6 I have studied French .... three months.

b

a

1 Write sentences comparing these two cars. You can use the words below and any other adjectives that you know.

old, new, large, small, expensive, cheap

Example Car A is older than car B.

2 Write the comparative form of these adjectives:

few .... safe .... big ....
kind .... close .... wet ....
plain .... gentle .... thin ....
dirty .... aggressive ....
lovely .... confident ....
pretty .... traditional ....
bad .... far ....
good-looking ....

3 Put the words in the sentences in the correct order.

Example bossier/is/than/her/Françoise/sister

Françoise is bossier than her sister.

1 men/ambitious/women/as/are/as

....

2 her/considerate/Susan/less/brother/than/is

....

3 not/busy/I/as/am/as/her

....

4 pretty/picture/as/she/as/is/a

....

5 more/you/confident/me/than/are

....

4 Complete the table.

Person	Job
nurse	*nursing*
plumber	
manager	
banker	
engineer	
lawyer	
teacher	
actress	

5 Odd one out? Which of the words doesn't belong?

1 pretty/attractive/kind/beautiful ....
2 considerate/selfish/generous/kind ....
3 pretty/lovely/beautiful/clean-cut ....
4 gentle/aggressive/bossy/selfish ....
5 electrician/nanny/plumber/car mechanic ....

6 Revision spot

Complete the story with the verbs below. Use the past simple and past continuous.

be, call, clean, repair, say, turn, wash

It ....¹ Sunday. Dad ....² the house, and Mum ....³ the car, and I ....⁴ the dog in the garden. Suddenly, my mother ....⁵ my father. 'Listen to this!' she ....⁶ proudly. She ....⁷ the key. 'I've fixed the car. It's working!'

PRACTICE SECTION

1 Do you know what these objects are? Read the text to find out more.

Boomerang-throwing has been popular among Australian Aborigines for thousands of years. Early Egyptians also used them for hunting. The first boomerangs were probably used for killing small animals like birds. Later
5 people started throwing them as a sport or pastime. Scientists have been interested in studying the aerodynamic design for many years.

If you decide to try boomerang-throwing, you should hold the boomerang over your shoulder and throw it
10 quickly into the air. You don't need to throw it very hard, but you need to move your wrist quickly. The boomerang will turn in the air, and return to you. I also suggest using a lightweight one at first: boomerangs can return very quickly and you could get a nasty bang on the head from a
15 heavy one.

If you would like to have more information, contact: The Boomerang Association, P.O. Box 155, Barooga, Victoria 3644, Australia.

How many gerunds and infinitives can you find in the text? Write them down.

2 Complete these sentences with a gerund or infinitive.

I'm scared of ....
I need ....
I'd like ....
I enjoy ....
I hate ....
I've decided ....

3 Read the clues and complete the crossword. Each answer is a word that can be used to describe a hobby.

Across

2 Learning a language is easy for some people, but d................. for others.
4 The film was so e................., I couldn't stop watching it.
5 This book isn't very interesting. In fact it is quite d..................
7 Some hobbies are so t.................. you don't have much time for other things.
8 I don't think I have enough money. It's very e................. isn't it?

Down

1 My job is very c.................. I have to try hard if I want to succeed.
2 Be careful. This path is d..................
3 Swimming is a very h. *ealthy* .... pastime for people of all ages.
6 After a hard day's work, I need to do something r..................

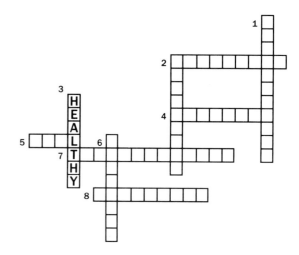

4 Write about hobbies and pastimes you are (not) interested in. Include:

– your favourite hobby or pastime.
– a hobby or pastime you would like to try and why.
– a hobby or pastime you wouldn't like to try and why.

5 Revision spot

a Fiona McFee has written this final checklist before she begins her journey. Write sentences about what she's *going to* do. Use these verbs:

buy, get, plan, put, write

batteries for torch ....
2 extra blankets ....
letters to her friends ....
her route ....
oil in oil lamp ....

b Write down your plans for the next three days. Use *going to* . . . .

....
....
....

(See exercise 4, p. 16). Student B: read this text and answer Student A's questions. Then ask him/her questions to find your missing information.

I didn't use to look like this; I created my own image. When I was a girl I used to look like everyone else. I enjoyed school. I used to be .... at school. But I hated .... You know, I could eat like a horse but I never got fat because I used to burn up so much energy. I was very good at .... , too. When I was at school in Jamaica, I wanted to become a language teacher but then in my early teens we moved to .... I was the only black girl in the school and I used to feel very strange. But it was there I learned about .... and that's when I became interested in singing. I suppose it was then, in my late teens, that I began to change .... When I was 13 or 14 people used to think I was about 35, now everybody thinks .... – I must be getting younger.

1 Using the text, write questions for these answers.

Example In Jamaica.

> *Where did she live before her family moved?*

1 When she was at school in New York.

   ....

2 Because she used to burn up so much energy.

   ....

3 Sitting still.

   ....

4 Because she was the only black girl in the school.

   ....

5 A language teacher.

   ....

2 **Put these words and phrases into the text.**

old-fashioned, fashionable, worn-out, do not have, did not have, wear, used to wear, wearing

Fashions change and people buy new clothes; not because their clothes are ....[1] but because they do not want to look ....[2]. In the old days, people used to keep the same clothes for years. Of course, many people ....[3] enough money to change their clothes every year. In many parts of the world, this is still true: people ....[4] the same style of clothes their grandparents ....[5]. This may be because people ....[6] enough money to buy new clothes or because they like ....[7] traditional dress. Certainly, being ....[8] is an expensive business.

3 Katherine Hamnett was voted Designer of the Year in 1984. Here are some details about her life. Write her biography in complete sentences.

Born	1947
Childhood	many countries with her parents – Sweden, France, Turkey
Education	boarding school in England – hated sport, loved art
Family	two boys aged 8 and 13 – divorced
Career	1979 – borrowed £500 to start new business – her kitchen was her studio
	1984 – Designer of the Year
	Now – top international designer
Diet	vegetarian food and home-made wine
Favourite countries	Italy – good for designers
	Spain – interesting and relaxing
Plans	open shop in Moscow

4 Put these words into the correct order to make phrases describing clothes.

Example green, a pair of, suede, shoes

> *a pair of green, suede shoes*

1 skirt, woollen, long, black, a ....

2 a, black, fitted, jacket, leather ....

3 a pair of, jeans, denim, tight ....

4 greenish, a, T-shirt, baggy ....

5 a, suede, skirt, black, straight ....

5 **Revision spot**

Complete the sentences with *have been/has been* or *has gone/have gone*.

1 I haven't seen you for a few days.
   No, I .... to the Paris Fashion Show. It was great.

2 Where are Anne and Sophie?
   They .... to town to buy some shoes.

3 We'd like to do an interview with Yazz.
   I'm sorry – she isn't here. She .... to the States.

4 .... you .... abroad?
   Yes, we .... to Jamaica. We got back yesterday.

5 .... Maria ....?
   Yes. She .... home to get her sweater.

1 **Write down the superlative form of these adjectives.**

rich .... close .... big ....
long .... late .... wet ....
poor .... gentle .... thin ....
bad .... good .... far ....

happy.................. convenient..................
pretty.................. disgusting..................
busy.................. interesting..................

2 **Use the information in the table to complete the statements. Use *more*, *less*, *fewer*, *the least* and *the fewest* in your statements.**

Most crowded countries (people per sq km)		Emptiest countries (people per sq km)	
Monaco	17,500	Western Sahara	0.5
Singapore	4,475	Mongolia	1.2
Vatican City	2,500	Botswana	1.8
Malta	1,266	Mauritania	1.8

Example Monaco is..... *the most*.. crowded country.

1 There are .... people per square km in Malta than in Singapore.
2 Vatican City is .... crowded than Singapore.
3 Singapore is .... crowded than Malta.
4 Western Sahara is .... crowded country.
5 It has .... number of people per sq km.

3 **Read the article and answer the questions that follow.**

Mt Blanc cut down to size

Europe's highest mountain was knocked down more than 10 feet yesterday. Mont Blanc, the Alpine peak which straddles France, Italy and Switzerland, has been accepted on maps as 15,872 feet high for years. But experts from the Italian army claim measurements using satellites now show it is only 15,862 feet high. Last year the military specialists said Mount Rose, the Alps' second highest peak, was 15,302 feet high instead of 15,312.

1 Which country discovered the mistake? How?
2 Which is higher, Mt Blanc or Mt Rose? By how many feet?

4 **Read the story. Then put the pictures in the correct order.**

The least successful nurse

In 1987, a student nurse saw an elderly woman sitting on the edge of a bed. 'Time for your bath,' said the nurse. 'I've already had one,' replied the old woman, who looked confused. The nurse led the old woman to her bath, took off her clothes and washed her thoroughly. When they returned to the ward, the nurse said, 'Someone else has got into your bed.' 'It's my sister,' replied the old lady. 'I've come to visit her.'

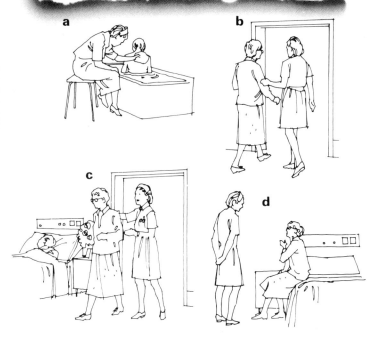

5 **Complete these sentences so they are true for you.**

1 My best friend's name is ....
2 My most beautiful item of clothing is ....
3 The farthest from home I have ever travelled was to
   ....
4 The kindest man/woman I know is ....
5 At school, my best subject is/was ....
6 My worst subject is/was ....

6 **Revision spot**

Write five sentences comparing people in your family using comparative adjectives.

Example My father is older than my mother.

....
....
....
....
....

10 PRACTICE SECTION

1

Put the verbs in the short conversations below into the *present perfect* or *present perfect continuous*.

1 A This is a nice pub. .... you
   .... (be) here before?
  B No, this is the first time.

2 A Where .... you .... (be)?
  B I .... (look) everywhere for a
    decent guidebook and I still .... (not
    find) one.

3 A How long .... you ....
    (smoke)?
  B Since I was a teenager.
  A Are you a heavy smoker?
  B Not really. I .... only ....
    (smoke) four or five today.

4 A What .... you .... (do)?
    You look tired.
  B My homework. I .... just ....
    (finish).

5 A Excuse me. .... you
    ....(wait) long?
  B Half an hour. There .... (be) an
    accident up the road and all the buses are running
    late.

2

Name one thing you might see or do in each of these places:

art gallery ....

museum ....

wilderness ....

pub ....

nightclub ....

restaurant ....

3

Find these adjectives in the dictionary and write the noun for each one.

adjective	noun
historic	*history*
enjoyable	
exciting	
interesting	
active	
colourful	
popular	

4

Read the advertisement for a holiday company, and complete it using these words and phrases. For some of the gaps more than one word is possible.

even more,   exciting,   golden,
interesting,   popular,   rare

Carousel have fast become a ....¹ choice for holidaymakers who want more for their money. At Carousel we sell great holidays at great value prices. And there is a growing number of ....² destinations to choose from. This summer there's ....³ to enjoy with the addition of Florida to the Carousel choice of holidays. Here the fun is larger than life. To the east and west are ....⁴ beaches. Further south are the Everglades, home to alligators and ....⁵ birds. All in all, Florida is one of the most ....⁶ holiday locations in the world!

5

Write a paragraph about a holiday you have taken. Include:

– where you went, and when.
– what you saw and did.
– what you liked and didn't like.

....

....

....

....

....

....

....

6 Revision spot

Write five sentences about what you *used to do* or *didn't use to do* when you went on holiday as a child.

Example When I was a child I used to play on the
         beach. I didn't use to play tennis.

....

....

....

....

....

....

....

1 **Complete the sentences using *who* or *which*.**

1 I have a friend .... drinks 10 cans of cola a day.
2 We live in a house .... is 300 years old.
3 Both coffee and tea contain caffeine, ... is highly addictive.
4 I like people .... are considerate.
5 I want to see the play .... is showing at the Palace.
6 Morocco is a place .... I would love to see.
7 Nicole is the girl .... sits next to me in English.

2 **Write an ending for these sentences.**

1 I can't stand people who ....
....
2 I have a friend who ....
....
3 I really like people who ....
....
4 I would like to meet someone who ....
....

3 **Use these words to finish the paragraph.**

addictive,   give up,   low,   which,   which

Why is chocolate so hard to ....¹? Because it gives you a quick shot of glucose ....² produces an instant lift to the spirits. Unfortunately, you'll suddenly feel ....³ an hour or so later. It also contains caffeine which is mildly ....⁴, and phenylethylamine, the same chemical ....⁵ our bodies produce when we are first madly in love with someone.

4 **These verbs are from the story about Maureen Harkavy. Write the noun for each one.**

Verb	Noun
threaten	
refuse	
warn	
pollute	
intend	
arrive	

5 **Match the questions in A with the best reply in B.**

A	B
1 Do you mind if I join you?	a I'd rather you didn't.
2 Can I borrow your pen?	b I'm afraid I'm not.
3 Would you like a coffee?	c Actually, I'm just leaving.
4 Do you mind if I turn on the television?	d I'm afraid I don't have one.
5 Are you free for lunch?	e No, thank you.

6 **Revision spot**

Complete the conversation with the verbs in brackets. Use the *present perfect* or *past simple*.

a .... you ever ....? (*fly*)
b Yes, many times. In fact, I .... as an airline steward until last year. (*work*)
c *Really? .... you ever .... about going back to it?* (*think*)
d Not really, but it .... fun at the time. (*be*)
e *I suppose you .... a lot of countries.* (*see*)
f Yes, I have.
g *Which one .... you .... the most?* (*like*)
h Do you want to know the truth? Britain. It .... always great to come home. (*be*)

"I worked as an airline steward"

1   Read the article and answer the questions.

Property boss gives £48 million to poor

Property emperor, Stephen Sander, is giving the world's poor a £48 million Christmas present.

Sander, 55, is transferring 80 percent of his company to a new charity foundation. It will produce an income of £632,000 a year for third-world relief projects.

The Sander empire includes 23 high-rise blocks in Vancouver, Canada. But he said, "Does anyone want two million dollars to live on? I don't, so why not work for other people?"

1 How much of his company is he giving away?
2 How much income will £48 million produce in two years?
3 Where does Stephen Sander own a lot of property?
4 Why is he giving the money to charity?

2 a Study the time-line of John Wright's life. Then complete the sentences using *when, while, before* or *after*. For some of the sentences there may be more than one correct answer.

- 1980 Second child born

- First child born
- 1976 | Started work as a primary school teacher
  | Finished university
- 1975 Got married

- 1971 – Started university

- 1954 – Born

1 He got married .... he was at university.
2 He was 21 .... he got married.
3 He got married .... he finished university.
4 .... he finished university, he taught in a primary school.
5 He started teaching .... his wife had their first child.
6 .... he was 26, they had their second child.

b Now write a paragraph about your own life using *when, while, before* and *after*.

3   Write the words connected with having or making money in the + column, and the words connected with not having or losing it in the − column.

credit, debit, debt, deposit, income, loss, overdraft, profit, save, spend, wages, withdraw

+	−

Can you add any more words to the columns?

4   Read the text and answer this question:

Why do you think the English words *cash* and *salary* are taken from the Indian and Latin words meaning tea and salt?

Did you know?

Coins and notes are not the only form of money. Teeth of animals, metal bracelets and necklaces, shells, axe heads, knives, blocks of salt and even blocks of tea leaves have been used. The word 'cash' comes from an Indian word meaning tea and the word 'salary' comes from the Latin word for salt.

Now read the answer at the bottom of the page.

5   **Revision spot**

Decide whether the verbs should be in the *present simple* or *present continuous*.

Dear Alex,

How ....¹ (be) you? Thanks for your letter. Sorry to be such a long time writing back, but I ....² (be) very busy these days. I ....³ (do) exams at the moment, and of course, I ....⁴ (study) very hard. I am happy to say that the business ....⁵ (do) very well – the term planners ....⁶ (be) very popular, indeed! In fact I ....⁷ (think) of expanding the business next year, after I ....⁸ (finish) college. I ....⁹ (think) term diaries could be a big success. What do you think? I ....¹⁰ (look forward) to seeing you when the exams ....¹¹ (be) all over!

Best wishes,
Peter

[Both were used to pay people in the past]

52

1 **Write sentences about these situations using** *when/ after + past perfect* **or** *when + past simple.*

Example
Your father went on a diet and stopped smoking at the same time.
When my father went on a diet, he stopped smoking.
Your mother went on a diet and then stopped smoking.
After my mother had been on a diet, she stopped smoking.

1 You did a few keep-fit classes and then started weightlifting.

....

2 Your friend went on a vegetarian diet and became ill at the same time.

....

3 You went skiing and broke your arm.
You broke your arm and then went to hospital.

....

....

4 Your parents stopped work and then began to put on weight.

....

2 **What is wrong with these people? Use the table to write sentences about them.**

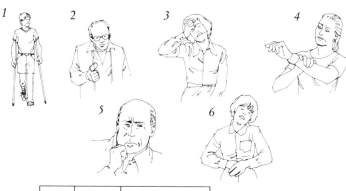

She He	's got	(a) . . . ache. a sore . . . a broken . . . a swollen . . .
	feels sick.	

3 **When was the last time you had a health problem? Write down the steps you took to get better.**

Example Last winter I had flu. First I went to the chemist to get some medicine. After I'd used it for a few days, I was no better, so I . . .

4 **Match the sentences in A with a suitable response in B.**

A
1 I'm afraid I can't come tomorrow. My mother's seriously ill in hospital.
2 Ouch! I've just cut my finger on a bread knife.
3 I haven't got a car now. I had an accident with a lorry yesterday.
4 I ate so much chocolate yesterday, I feel really ill.

B
a Oh dear. Let me get you a plaster.
b My goodness. That's terrible! How did it happen?
c Oh, no. I'm very sorry to hear that.
d Well, it serves you right.

5 **Look at the phrases you found for giving advice in exercise 5 (p. 26). Write down the advice you would give to these people, using the phrases you have learned.**

1 A friend at work has just had a serious accident.

....

2 Someone who smokes a lot has a very serious cough.

....

3 A friend complains about putting on a lot of weight.

....

4 Your father has just come out of hospital, and he is thinking of going back to work already.

....

5 A friend of yours is always tired and has no energy.

....

6 Someone in your class suddenly says to you, 'I don't feel very well'.

....

6 **Revision spot**

Write the correct form of the verb in brackets in the sentences. Use the *present perfect simple* **or** *present perfect continuous.*

Example Ouch! I ......*'ve cut*.... (*cut*) my finger.

1 Oh, my fingers hurt. I .... (*type*) all day.
2 My father is so tired. He .... (*work*) really hard these last two months.
3 She's very fit. She .... (*train*) for years.
4 They .... (*go*) to hospital to visit their mother.
5 Medical scientists .... (*try*) to find a cure since the 1960s.

1 Look at the pictures and write sentences using *must, mustn't, should* and *shouldn't.*

Example a *You shouldn't leave toys on stairs.*

b ....

c ....

d ....

e ....

f ....

2 Use the words below to complete the paragraph.

have, never, if, when, must, always, when, try, never, look around, plan,

.................¹ you drive at night, ...² to keep to main well-lit roads. ....³ your route in advance and ....⁴ enough money and petrol to get there and back. ....⁵ be wary of hitch-hikers and ....⁶ you see someone you think needs help, ...⁷ leave your car unless you are sure it's a genuine emergency. Park in well-lit areas and ....⁸ before you leave your car. ....⁹ leave valuables in the car, but if you ....¹⁰ leave something behind, lock it in the boot. ....¹¹ you return to the car quickly check the inside before you get in, and have your car key ready.

3 Finish these sentences with *if* or *when.*

1 .... I live to be 100, I'm going to have a huge party.

2 I'm going to move to Spain .... I retire.

3 .... you've finished what you're doing, can you give me a hand?

4 .... you lose your handbag, contact the police immediately.

5 .... I finish studying English, I'm going to learn Italian.

6 What will you do .... you pass your exam?

7 .... someone bothers you on a train, complain to the guard.

8 .... we ruin the environment, we'll never forgive ourselves.

4 Write the word for the criminal beside the crime.

Crime	Criminal
robbery shoplifting murder smuggling mugging burglary blackmail	*a robber*

Now add more crimes and criminals to the list.

5 **Revision spot**

Complete the sentences with the correct form of the words in brackets.

1 If you .... (*not careful*), you'll get burnt.

2 If you're going to be late, ... you .... (*phone*) me?

3 If you .... (*not hurry*), we'll be late.

4 If we leave now, we .... just .... (*catch*) the train.

5 If the weather .... (*not improve*), we .... (*have to*) cancel the picnic.

6 If you .... (*not study*), you .... (*not pass*) your exams.

7 If I .... (*see*) Clare, I .... (*invite*) her to the party.

8 If I .... (*finish*) work early, I .... (*ring*) you.

1 Put these verbs into the correct place in the text, in the *present passive*.

destroy,   throw away,   kill,   use,   cut down

Many of our animals are in danger of extinction: for example, leopards and tigers which are hunted for their beautiful furs and the African elephant which ....[1] for its ivory tusks. Other animals, like gorillas, are in danger when the forests ....[2] and the land ....[3] for new roads and towns. Most animals cannot survive when their homes ....[4]. Rats are the exception. They live on the rubbish which .... [5] every day, all over the world.

2 Match the descriptions of these items with the pictures. Then put the verb in brackets into the correct form of the passive.

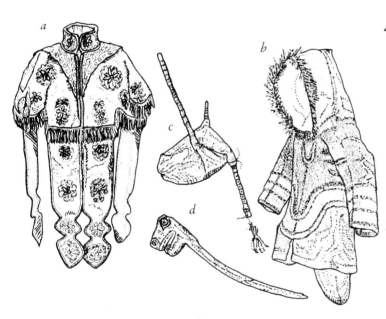

1 This jacket ..*was made*.. (make) in the last century by an Inuit woman. Sealskins .... (sew) together to make a warm coat.

2 Many years ago these sticks .... (use) by native Americans as part of a trap to catch small animals. The stick .... (make) from whalebone and a wolf's head .... (carve) on the top.

3 This musical instrument comes from Bulgaria. It .... (make) from goatskin. The three pipes .... (fix) to the neck and the two front legs of the animal's skin.

4 From 1941 to 1974, Ethiopia .... (rule) by Emperor Haile Selassie. His jacket .... (decorate) with part of a lion's mane.

3 Put these phrases and sentences into the dialogue.

As far as I'm concerned ...
... you're right.
... I'm not so sure.
... I don't think we should ...
... I agree.

– I think animals are great for children.
Yes, ...*I agree*......
– ....[1] I think all children should have pets.
Oh, ...[2] What about children who live in the centre of town in small flats?
– But you can get small pets like birds.
Oh, no ....[3] keep birds in cages, they should be free.
– Yes, I suppose ....[4].

4 Write a paragraph about your opinions of one of the topics in exercise 5 (p. 30). Write:

1 your opinion and why you think so. (I think/don't think we should, because ...)
2 an opposite opinion which you have heard but disagree with. (Some people say ...)
3 why you disagree with it. (but I disagree with that because ...)
4 your final opinion (As far as I'm concerned ...)

5 Revision spot

Put these adjectives into the correct form in the sentences.

long,   large,   ugly,   dangerous,   expensive

Example
A cheetah can run at 110 kmph, this means it is probably *the fastest* animal in the world.

1 The .... land animal is the African elephant at about 10 metres long from tail to trunk.
2 Leopard skin is one of the .... furs you can buy. One small coat costs thousands of pounds.
3 The American vampire bat is the .... bat in the world. It can give people several diseases when it sucks blood.
4 The land animal with the .... life expectancy is the Asiatic elephant. It can live to 80 years old.
5 The South American jumping spider has four eyes and a black and brown hairy face. It is one of the .... insects in the world.

1 Read the text and:

- underline all the direct speech.
- write sentences changing the direct speech to indirect speech.
- write a list of the verbs you changed from direct to indirect speech.

direct speech	indirect speech

23-year-old ski champion, Vaila McDonald enjoys both climbing and skiing. She decided to try the two sports together when she went on an expedition to the Himalayas with four friends. 'I have always wanted to
5 go to the Himalayas and no-one has ever skied down Mera Peak before,' Vaila explained. She enjoyed the expedition but they had a few problems. 'I am not really a mountain climber,' she said. 'I got a terrible headache from the altitude.' They lost their tents in a
10 blizzard and had to shelter under a rock where they huddled together all night to keep warm. 'I was terrified,' Vaila said. Although the weather was terrible she skied to the bottom of the mountain. Now she's keen to go on another expedition. 'I'm going to go to
15 the ski championships in Europe in March,' she explained. 'And then, I'll go somewhere in Nepal; somewhere that no-one has ever been to before.'

2 Read the text in exercise 1 again and find the words that mean the following:

1 An organised journey, made by several people usually to a place far away is an ....
2 The .... of a place is its height above sea level.
3 A very bad snow storm with strong winds is a ....
4 People .... together usually because they are cold or frightened.
5 If you are .... you are very frightened.

3 These are some of the comments Vaila made before going on the expedition. Change them to direct speech.

1 Vaila said she was a good skier but not an expert climber.

....

2 Vaila told us she loved skiing and climbing, but she was a little afraid of going to the Himalayas.

....

....

3 Vaila said she had never been so high before.

....

4 She told us the experienced climbers would help her.

....

5 She said she hoped the weather was going to be fine.

....

4 Read this interview with Stephan Nilson, Swiss champion of semi-contact. (A martial art, like Kung Fu or Karate.) Then write a newspaper article describing:

- why he started the sport.
- his training.
- which countries do the sport.
- his ambitions.

I: Why did you start this sport?
S: Well, I've always been interested in martial arts, and I enjoy the training you do for semi-contact.
I: How often do you train?
S: Oh, about 6–10 hours a week.
I: Do many countries do semi-contact?
S: Not really. It's popular in the USA, Britain, Germany and a few other European countries.
I: And would you like to be world champion?
S: Yes, I would like the title of course, but I'm more interested in enjoying sport than in being a world champion.

5 Revision spot

Write these sentences putting the verb in brackets into the *gerund* or the *infinitive*.

1 Vaila is interested in .... (*go*) to Nepal. She would like .... (*go*) there next year.
2 'I love .... (*ski*) but I'm not very good at .... (*climb*),' Vaila told us.
3 Not many people in the class are keen on .... (*learn*) how to play cricket.
4 Dave liked .... (*cycle*) when he was younger. Then he decided .... (*try*) skateboarding.
5 I hate .... (*do*) outdoor sports in winter.

PRACTICE SECTION

1 a Write down some rules for your ideal school like this:

Compulsory	Not compulsory	Forbidden
to arrive on time	to wear a uniform	to smoke in class

b **Write about the rules and regulations and add your reasons.**

Example
In my ideal school, students have to arrive at school on time because if they arrive late they disturb the other students.

2 **Match the subjects on the left with their area of study on the right.**

Biology		the mind.
Chemistry		living things.
Crafts		beliefs.
Economics	is	how societies are organised.
Environmental Studies	the	substances.
Linguistics	study	how money is organised.
Philosophy	of	how languages work.
Psychology		the natural world.
Religious Studies		ideas and ways of thinking.
Social Science		making things by hand.

3 **Write down three skills you have**

Example I can …
    I know how to …

....
....
....

Then write down three skills you would like to have and say why.

Example
I don't know how to swim. I'd like to learn because it's good for your health and it could save your life.

....
....
....

4 Write four paragraphs about your school experiences. Write in the past or the present.

In paragraph 1 write:
– when you started school
– how long you spent/will spend there
– what the school was/is like

In paragraph 2 write:
– some of the things you had/have to do/weren't/aren't allowed to do
– what you thought/think about these rules
– some of the things you are/were allowed to do
– what you thought/think about that

In paragraph 3 write:
– the things you like(d) and why
– the things you dislike(d) and why
– what kind of student you were/are

In paragraph 4 write:
– what you think were/are the most important things you learned and why
– what kind of school you think is best for students and why

5 **Revision spot**

Put the verb in brackets into the correct form of the *passive*.

Summerhill, a very progressive school in the south of England, ...[1] (*started*) in the 1960s by A. S. Neill. He believed that many children were not interested in what they ....[2] (*teach*) by their teachers and that children ....[3] (*give*) a lot of dos and don'ts which were completely unnecessary.
The school still exists today. It is a boarding school but parents ....[4] (*invited*) to visit the school when they want. Children ....[5] (*not tell*) which lessons they have to go to; they are allowed to choose to attend a lesson or not. Students at the school ....[6] (*ask*) if they agree with the rules of the school and they are allowed to vote on all school rules. Even today, this school ....[7] (*describe*) in many books which discuss alternative types of education and in the 1960s and 70s, Summerhill ....[8] (*use*) as a model for many schools in the USA. Of course, the school ....[9] (*criticise*) by many people who do not agree with its methods.

1 Use the table to help you write predictions about the 21st century. Then make up some of your own.

In ten years' time, I
| will |
| might | be married.
| may | have children.
| won't | have the same job.

By the year 2050, people
| will probably | live on Mars.
| probably won't | own robots.

2 Number the sentences in the correct order, to make a paragraph.

a Since 1984, scientists have been looking into the use of 'magic bullets' to cure cancer.

b But the healing potential of 'magic bullets' doesn't end there.

c 'Magic bullets' find and destroy cancer cells without harming the healthy cells around them.

d They may also be used as a vaccine against diseases like AIDS and the common cold.

e One of the big stories of the 90s may be that science has finally found a cure for cancer. (1)

3 Write the words and phrases in their correct place on the line.

will probably,   may,   will,   probably won't,
will certainly,   won't,   certainly won't

Certainty — a ....

— b will ....

— c ....

Uncertainty — d ....

— e ....

— f ....

Certainty — g ....

4 Match the words and prefixes in A with the words in B that they relate to.

A	B
micro	numbers
solar	the moon
digital	water
thermal	very small
mega	movement
lunar	the sun
hydro	very large
mobile	heat

5 Complete these definitions of words from the unit by writing the words out in full.

1 A c........ is something which makes a disease go away.

2 A v.......... is something which prevents people from getting a disease.

3 A r........ is a machine which does things automatically.

4 The e.............. is the natural world.

5 L.......... time is time when you are not working and can enjoy yourself.

6 You have a s........ if the sun has made your skin brown.

6 Revision spot

Complete the sentences with *will* (*'ll*) or *going to*.

1 A The phone's ringing.
  B I .... answer it.

2 A What are your plans for this evening?
  B I .... watch television.

3 A Ouch, I've cut my finger.
  B Wait there. I .... get you a plaster.

4 A Have you done your homework yet?
  B No, but I .... do it this afternoon.

5 A Where are you going for your holiday this year?
  B America. I .... rent a car and drive around California.

(See exercise 2, p. 37). Student B: Use the information about Suresh to answer Student A's questions. Then ask Student A questions to complete your text about Suhartono.

Text B Suhartono

Suhartono comes from ..... He is .... years old and lives with his parents in a house made of .... with a ....floor. The house has no .... or ....; the family has to use the river as a lavatory. The family own .... land and their only possessions are ...., ..., ..., ..., ... and a ...... His father is a .... and earns ..... If he could afford it he would .....

Suresh:

Age:	8	*Place of birth:*	Nepal
Father's job:	labourer	*Income:*	£13 a month
Family house:	made of mud and stone, a straw roof, cook with a wood fire, no water and no sanitation		
Possessions:	some cooking pots, a bed, no land		
With more money:	send Suresh to school		

1 Write a paragraph about Suresh from the table above, without looking at the text in the Student's book.

2 Write about what you would do if you won a) £10,000, b) £100,000, c) £1 million. Write down:

– how you would spend the money.
– how your life would/wouldn't change.
– how much you would give away.
– if you think you would be a happier person.

Write a paragraph for each of the three amounts of money.

3 a Put these words into the correct place in the text.

money, expensive, charity, luxury, well-off, precious stones, percentage, wealthy, price, luxurious

American dogs can live a life of ....[1] if their owners are very ....[2]. A company in New York called Animal Manors has started to design dog kennels which are more ....[3] than some people's houses. These architect-designed kennels come with window boxes with real flowers, oriental carpets and soft cushions. Owners who are not so ....[4] can pay the minimum ....[5] of $475

and the better-off can pay as much as $10,000 for their dog's home. There is even a very ....[6] model which they sell at $200,000 which is made from gold, silver and ....[7]. The company says that the customers need not worry about spending so much ....[8] on a dog kennel, because they give a small ....[9] of every sale to a ....[10] – to help under-privileged dogs!

b Have you ever seen a very expensive object which you thought was a waste of money? Describe the object, say how much it cost and why you thought it was a waste of money.

4 **Revision spots**

a **Put this text into indirect speech.**

My name is Leila and I come from Aswan in Egypt. I am fifteen years old and have to leave school now, because my parents want me to work with them in the market. I am going with my father to Cairo soon. I think I'll enjoy the trip very much because I've never been outside Aswan before.

Start like this:

She said her name was . . .

b **Read the text.**

In northern India, many families find it difficult to live from farming alone. Often, the men are forced to find jobs in the nearest city to earn extra money. They can be away from home for many months of the year. This means the women are responsible for all the farming, bringing up the children and looking after the home.

For many of the children in the area, school is an hour's journey away. The walk over steep mountains is too long and difficult for very young children. Recently, day centres (balwadi) have been set up for the young children. The centres offer opportunities for play and learning so that children are more likely to go on to primary school. The balwadi have become so popular that many women want them for their older children too.

Write sentences about what the men, women and children:

– have to do.
– had to do before the balwadi.

Example The men have to find jobs in the cities.

1 Finish these sentences. Use one of the time expressions below.

next month/year, last month/year,
at the end of the week/month/year,
by the time I'm . . .

Example I'm going to go to Spain *next year*.

1 I wanted to ....
2 I'm going to ....
3 I don't plan to ....
4 I'd like to ....
5 I'll probably ....

2 Complete these definitions of words from the unit by writing the words out in full.

1 A q............ is a characteristic of a person such as kindness or honesty.
2 A t........ is a rich, powerful person.
3 To a............ someone is to like them very much.
4 A f............ is a serious food shortage.
5 An important problem is an i......... .
6 A d........ course is a course which teaches you to plan and draw things.

3 The teenagers in the survey (see exercise 2 p. 39) said that the following things would be most important when they were thirty:

relationships	41%
career	29%
having fun	22%
freedom	8%

What do you think will be most important to you when you are 40/50/70/100? Write a sentence for each age.

Example
When I'm 40, my family will be most important to me.

....
....
....
....

4 Complete the questions with the correct question words.

1 .... have you lived here? – Three years.
2 .... did you finish college? – Last year.
3 .... longer are you going to stay here? – Another year.
4 .... have you been studying English? – Since September.
5 .... are you going to start your new job? – Tomorrow.

5 Revision spot

a Read this and mark the statements about the speaker as true or false. Correct the false statements.

'I'd definitely like to move out of London and back to Scotland. I'd like to live somewhere that is better for the children to grow up in. I can't see myself doing the same sort of work as I've been doing. I'll probably give up my job because I'd like to do more work at home. And I'm definitely not going to have any more children.'

1 She wants to leave London.	T/F
2 She probably won't move to Scotland.	T/F
3 She's going to give up her job.	T/F
4 She may do more of her work at home.	T/F
5 She won't have any more children.	T/F

b Complete the sentences with *who* or *which*.

I have a friend ....[1] lives in Scotland. She lives in a house ....[2] is 200 years old. She bought it from an old man ....[3] couldn't look after it any more. It had stairs ....[4] were too difficult for him to climb and a garden ....[5] was too large for him to keep.

Grammar reference

Unit 1

The present simple

1 The present simple is used in two main ways:
a) to talk about true facts not connected to a special time.
English *contains* about 5,000,000 technical words.
Some Welsh people *do not speak* English.
Does it rain a lot in Japan?
b) to talk about habits or repeated events.
In my job I *write letters* in French, Spanish and German.
She *doesn't usually speak* Chinese at school.
Do you often go to Italy?

2 The present simple uses the auxiliary verb *do* and *does* in questions and negatives. *Do* is used when the subject is **I**, **you**, **we** or **they**, and *does* is used when the subject is **he**, **she** or **it**. Be very careful to use *do* or *does* when the subject is **they** or **it**.

What does *this word* mean?	subject = it
Which languages do *people in Nigeria* speak?	subject = they
Thousands of London children do not speak English as their first language.	subject = they
This dictionary does not contain many scientific words.	subject = it

3 The auxiliaries *do* and *does* are not used with certain verbs:
a) **be** Are you married? Is he French? I'm not Italian.
b) **modal verbs:** *can, could, must, should.*
Could we have . . .? You shouldn't do that. She can't write.
c) **have got** Have you got any money? She hasn't got a car.
When **have** is used without **got** it needs *do* and *does*.
What time *do you have* breakfast? This dictionary *does not have* any American spellings.

Unit 2

Modals

1 *Can, could, will* and *would* are called modal auxiliary verbs. So are: *shall, should, may, might, ought to* and *must*. Modals are always followed by an infinitive without *to*.
I must go . . . He will come . . .

2 Modal verbs are different from other verbs in three ways:
a) they do not have *-s, -ing*, or *-ed* endings.
I can swim . . .   He can swim . . .
b) they come before the subject in questions.
Will you meet me at 6 o'clock?
c) they come before *not (n't)* in negative sentences.
I can't remember her name . . .
Note that *can't, won't* and *shan't* are often used instead of *cannot, will not* and *shall not*.

3 a) To make requests with **you** we can use *can, could, will* or *would*:
Can/Could/Will/Would you bring the cheque please?
b) To make requests with **I**, only *can* and *could* can be used:
Can/Could I borrow your pen?
c) Requests with *would* and *could* are generally more formal than requests with *can* and *will*.

4 a) Offers can be made with *can, could* and *would*:
Can/Could I get you some more coffee?
Would you like some more coffee?
b) **Note that** *I'd like* . . . is a polite way of asking for something, while *I (don't) like* . . . is used to talk about likes and dislikes:
I'd like a cup of coffee, please.   = a polite request
I like coffee, but I don't like tea.   = describing likes

Unit 3

The past simple and the past continuous

1 The past simple is used to talk about events which happened at a definite point in the past.
He took this photograph twenty years ago.
What did he do when *he saw* the strange light in the sky?
I didn't see any monsters when *I went* to Scotland.
All these events are completed actions in the past.

2 The past simple takes the auxiliary verb *did* + the infinitive of the verb for questions and negative statements.

positive	negative	question
I saw	I didn't see	Did you see . . .?
He took	He didn't take	Did he take . . .?

3 The past continuous is used to talk about:
a) temporary events in the past.
When I met him he *was living* in Paris.
(i.e. Maybe he is living somewhere else now)
The Berlin Symphony Orchestra *were playing* in Paris last week.
(i.e. They don't always play in Paris)
b) interrupted actions.
What *were you doing* when the fire started?
I *was watching* TV when I heard a strange noise.
c) describing the background to a story.
The sun *was shining*, birds *were singing* and I *was feeling* quite happy when I left home that day.

4 Notice the difference between the past simple and the past continuous in these questions and answers.
1 *What was he doing* when he heard the strange noise?
He *was watching* TV.
2 *What did he do* when he heard the strange noise?
He *switched* all the lights *off* in the living room.

Unit 4

Going to and *will*

1   There are several ways of talking about the future. One of the most important is *going to + the infinitive* of the verb. *Going to . . .* is usually used for:
a) future intentions.
> What are you *going to do* this weekend?
> They are *going to take the exam next June*.
Note that *going to . . .* can be used for the near future or the distant future.
b) predictions.
> It's *going to rain* soon.
> I'm afraid he *isn't going to pass* the exam.

2   When talking about future plans, you can also use the present continuous.
> I'*m taking* the exam in June.
This means you have registered, know the date, etc.

3   *Will + infinitive* is also used for the future. One of its uses is to talk about decisions made at the time of speaking.
> Are you leaving now? I think *I'll come* with you.
> It's quite late, *we'll get* a taxi.
In these types of example *will* is only used with **I** or **we** because it is a personal decision.

4   The negative of *will* in spoken English is *won't*.
> No, I *won't go* just now. We *won't get* a taxi, we'll walk.
For some other uses of *will* see Units 12, 18 and 19.

Unit 5

Present perfect and past simple

1   The present perfect is formed with *to have* (*have* or *has*) + past participle. Most past participles are formed by adding *-ed* (worked, lived), but some are irregular (been, gone).
> I/You/We/They have(n't) lived there.
> He/She has(n't) lived there.
> Have you/we/they (ever) lived abroad?
> Has he/she (ever) lived abroad?
> Yes, I have./he/she has.
> No, I haven't./never have./he/she hasn't.

2   The past simple is used to talk about the past, and the present perfect is used when there is a link between past and present.
> He was here last night/week/yesterday/a day/a week ago.
In this example the time is definitely past.
> He's been here since 1981.
In this example there is a link between past and present i.e. from 1981 to now.
> He has been/was here for ten days.
With *has been* = he is still here.
With *was* = he has now gone.

3   The present perfect is used with *ever* to mean *in your life* and with *never* to mean *never in your life*.
> Have you *ever been* to Spain? (Ever in your life?)
> No, never. (Never in my life.)

4   The present perfect is used with *gone* to mean the person has not yet come back.
> He's *gone* to the shops (and he's still there).
The present perfect is used with *been* to mean the person has gone and come back.
> He's *been* to the shops (but he's back now).

Unit 6

Adjectives in comparisons

1   Adjectives
a) Adjectives tell us something about a noun.
> *pretty*, *blue* dresses
Dresses is a noun and *pretty* and *blue* tell you about them.
b) Adjectives can come:
> – before a noun: She is an *intelligent* woman.
> – after certain verbs e.g. *be*, *seem* or *look*: She is *intelligent*.

2   Comparisons
a) The comparative form of short adjectives is *-er*.
> short – shorter   tall – taller   happy – happier
Less can be used with short adjectives, but this is not common.
b) We use *more* and *less* with longer adjectives.
> He's more/less intelligent than her.
c) (*Not*) *as + adj + as* can be used to show that two things are equal/not equal.
> Jane is *as tall as* Sue. (They're the same height.)
> She is *not as tall as* me. (We're not the same height.)
d) Some irregular adjectives are:
> good – better   bad – worse   far – farther/further

Unit 7

Gerunds and infinitives

1   Verbs followed by the infinitive: *would like, want, decide*
> I *decided to try* photography. He *wants to learn* Spanish.
> They *would like to have* a different teacher.

2   Verbs followed by the gerund: *enjoy, fancy, suggest*
> Do you *enjoy dancing*? I *don't fancy going out* tonight. What do you *suggest doing*?

3   Verbs followed by the infinitive *or* the gerund:
a) *like, love*
> I *love to sleep/sleeping* under the stars in the open air.
> Do you *like to travel/travelling* alone?
Both gerund and infinitive are possible in these sentences but the gerund is more common.
Would love . . . takes the infinitive.
> I'*d love to come* with you to Paris.
b) *like, hate*
When speaking about things in general these usually take the gerund.
> My son *hates dancing* but he *likes going* to concerts.

When these verbs mean (*don't*) *want*, they take the infinitive.

I *don't like to tell you* this but I have to.

I *hate to wake you up* but it's time to go.

c) *need*

With a person as subject, *need* usually takes an infinitive.

You *need to practise* a lot.

We *don't need to book* a table.

With a thing as subject, it usually takes the gerund.

This cinema *needs cleaning*.

My hair *needs cutting*.

d) *intend*

Intend can be followed by an infinitive *or* a gerund.

We *intend to see/seeing* the new Polish film.

Intend + infinitive is more common for future intentions. When an intention was not carried out it is usual to use *intended + gerund*.

We *intended seeing* it but we didn't have time.

4 The gerund is used after prepositions.

to be interested in/scared of/good/bad at/keen on doing . . .

Unit 8

Used to . . .

1 *Used to . . . + infinitive* is used to talk about:

a) the past being different from now.

Grace Jones *used to live* in Jamaica.

What *did she use to do* before she became a singer?

I *didn't use to be* quiet. When I was a child I was noisy.

b) a habit or repeated action in the past which does not happen now.

She *used to smoke* 40 cigarettes a day.

(Either she smokes less now or she doesn't smoke.)

My grandmother *used to milk* the cows every morning.

(But she doesn't any longer.)

I always *used to go camping* with my parents when I was a child.

All these examples happened repeatedly or over a long period of time. It is not possible to say:

* I used to get married in 1985.

This is one single action in the past and would be:

I got married in 1985.

If someone was married and is now divorced, you can say:

I used to be married.

2 **Note that** the question and negative form of *used to . . .* is the same as other verbs in the past:

did they use to . . ., we *didn't* use to . . .

The letter **d** is omitted.

Unit 9

Superlative adjectives

1 The superlative form of short adjectives is: *adjective + est*.

short – shorter – the shortest   happy – happier – the happiest

2 *Most* and *least + adj* are used with longer adjectives.

expensive – more/less expensive – the most/least expensive

3 Some adjectives are irregular:

good – better – best   bad – worse – worst   far – further – farthest

4 *The least* is used in front of mass nouns and *the fewest* in front of countable nouns.

the least money   the fewest people

See Grammar Reference, Unit 6 for notes on comparative adjectives.

Unit 10

Present perfect simple and continuous

1 The form of the present perfect continuous is:

I/You/We/They have been doing.

He/She/It has been doing.

Have	you	been doing?	Yes,	I have.
Has	he/she			he has.
			No,	I haven't.
				he hasn't.

2 The present perfect continuous is used to talk about:

a) actions or events that started in the past, continued, and are happening now.

I've been living here for two years.

b) to stress that a recent event has continued for some time.

It's been raining.

3 The present perfect simple can be used to describe an action that is repeated.

I've taken 20 photos of Westminster Abbey.

4 In many cases the present perfect simple can be used instead of the present perfect continuous.

I have worked/have been working here for 20 years.

Note: See Unit 5 for notes on the present perfect simple.

Unit 11

Defining relative clauses with *who* and *which*

1 Relative pronouns are used to join two sentences. They can be either the subject or object in the relative clause:

a) subject: The woman is blind. *She* answered the door.

The woman *who* answered the door is blind.

b) object: It was an experience. I'll never forget *it*.

It was an experience *which* I'll never forget.

2 When you want to use a relative pronoun to refer to a person or groups of people, you use *who*.

> . . . *the woman who* answered the door.

3 When you want to use a relative pronoun to refer to a thing or group of things, you use *which*.

> . . . *an experience which* I'll never forget.

Unit 12
Revision of tenses

1 The *past simple* is used to refer to events which took place at a definite time in a person's past:

> *When he was 15, he signed his schoolmates up* . . .

It can also be used to refer to a habit or a state which took place in the past:

> *I felt* that the planners were pretty unimaginative.

2 The *present simple* is used to refer to present states or habits in a person's life:

> Now, Peter Blackburn *is* Managing Director . . . (state).
> He *keeps in touch* with his headquarters (habit).

3 To emphasise that the event was/is temporary, the *past* or *present continuous* is used:

> At five, he *was collecting* old newspapers . . .

4 When we make predictions or state our opinion about events in the future, *will/won't* can be used:

> . . . my company *will support* me next year.

Phrases like 'He reckons' or 'He thinks' show that you are not absolutely certain about what you are saying.

> He reckons it will show a profit of more than £15,000. (That is his opinion, but he is not absolutely sure.)

When, while, before, after

1 *Before* and *after* show the order of events when the same person does two actions.

> Before he set up the company, he spent . . .

2 *When* shows that something happened at a particular time.

> When he was 15, . . .

3 *While* shows that two things happened at the same time.

> While fellow students are out with their friends, he keeps in touch . . .

Unit 13
The past perfect

1 When talking about events in the past we sometimes need to emphasise that one event happened before another. This can be done by using the past perfect.

> She stopped smoking. She went on a diet
> = When she *had stopped* smoking she *went* on a diet.

If both verbs in this sentence are in the past simple, it means that the two events happened at the same time.

> = When she *stopped* smoking she *went* on a diet.

2 The difference can also be made clear by using *after* or

before instead of *when*. Then the past simple can be used instead of the past perfect.

> After she stopped/had stopped smoking she went . . .
> She stopped/had stopped smoking before she went . . .

Both past simple and past perfect are possible here but the past perfect is often used to give more emphasis.

3 It is sometimes difficult to hear the word *had* in spoken English because it is pronounced **'d**.

> I'd decided to try weight training before I saw the gym.

4 Occasionally the use of the past perfect is very important to the meaning of the sentence.

> a) When he arrived at the party she left.
> b) When he arrived at the party she had left.

Sentence a suggests that she did not want to see him and left because he arrived. *Sentence b* means she left before he came and his arrival and her leaving may not be connected.

Unit 14
If and *when* in the zero conditional

1 You can use *when* to talk about events that are likely or certain to happen.

> When you are at home, keep your doors locked.
> When you've finished, give me a call.

2 You can use *if* to talk about events that could or might happen.

> If you feel you are threatened, scream and run.
> If you are at all worried, call the police.

3 Although both *if* and *when* can be used to refer to events in the future, they are not used with *will*. You do **not** say:

> ⁕ If you will feel threatened, . . . or
> ⁕ When you will be at home, . . .

The imperative

With sentences beginning with *if* and *when* to give advice or warnings, the second half of the sentence is often in the imperative. That means that the subject (you) is not stated, and the verb is in the present simple tense.

> When you are at home, *keep your doors locked*.
> If you feel you are threatened, *call the police*.

Unit 15
The passive in the present and past simple

1 The passive is used when you do not know, or are not interested in, who performed a particular action.

> Thousands of whales *are killed* each year.

It is not **who** killed the whales that is of interest. The interest is in the whales and the fact that they have been killed (by someone).

2 The passive = *be + past participle* of the main verb.

> Whale meat *is given* . . ./Whales *are killed* . . .
> He *was found* . . ./The children *were taken* . . .

Be must be in its correct form i.e. singular/plural, past/present etc. depending on what the subject of the verb is.

3 Past participles of regular verbs are formed by adding *-ed* to the infinitive of the verb.

kill – killed   clean – cleaned   repair – repaired

The past participles of irregular verbs are formed in various different ways and have to be learned.

take – taken   find – found   put – put   steal – stolen

Unit 16

Direct and indirect speech

1 Special punctuation is needed for people's exact words.
He said, "My favourite sports are swimming and tennis."

When speaking you do not usually want to repeat the exact words, so indirect speech is used.
He said (that) his favourite sports were swimming and tennis.

Notice the changes: my – his   are – were

2 The verb tenses are often different when changing from direct to indirect speech. Notice these verb changes:

"My name is . . ."		her name was . . .
"I studied . . ."		she had studied . . .
"I can't play badminton."		she couldn't play badminton.
"I'll try to learn."	She said	she would try to learn.
"I've never done any sport."		she had never done any sport.
"I'm going to start again soon."		she was going to start again soon.

3 When facts in a reported statement are still true at the time of speaking, the verb tenses do not need to be changed: they may be changed but it is not necessary.

"My name is . . ."		her name is . . .
"I come from . . ."	She said	she comes from . . .
"I broke my leg . . ."		she broke her leg . . .

4 Sometimes *that* is used to introduce a reported statement.
She said *that* her name was . . .

The word *that* can be included or not, without changing the meaning of the sentence.

Unit 17

Have to and *be allowed to* . . . (obligation)

1 *Have to* . . . is similar in meaning to *must* . . .
All pupils have to/must wear a uniform.

The negative of *have to* . . . is different in meaning from the negative of *must* . . . .

1 Pupils *must not leave* school before their sixteenth birthday.

= Pupils are not allowed to leave school at 15.

2 Pupils *do not have to leave* school after their sixteenth birthday.

= Pupils can leave at 16 or continue at school after 16.

2 There is no past tense form of *must*: it is necessary to use *had to* . . .

Today most pupils *must/have to learn* about computers but they don't have to wear uniforms. When I was at school, we *had to wear* a uniform, but we didn't have to learn about computers. Did you have to do the same?

There is no past tense form of *must not*: *was/were not allowed to* . . . is often used.

We *weren't allowed to* smoke at my school. Even today in many schools the pupils *mustn't* smoke.

3 In spoken British English, it is possible to find *have got to* instead of *have*.

I'm sorry I can't, *I've got to do* my homework.

Unit 18

Certainty and uncertainty

1 *Will/won't* can be used to show certainty about future events.
Nancy will arrange it.

Note that *shall/shan't* can be used with the first person to show strong certainty about the future or strong intention.
I shall make a lot of money one day.

2 When a future event is uncertain, *may* can be used.
They may come later.

3 *Probably* can be used for an event that is likely to happen, but is still uncertain.
They'll probably be late./They probably won't go.

Notice the position of *probably* in both sentences.

4 There are many other words or phrases that show the certainty of a future event:
Perhaps they'll come early.
It's *possible/likely* that they won't come at all.

Unit 19

If sentences in first and second conditional

1 Statements with *if* usually contain two distinct parts; each part has its own verb. The verb in the first part often has a different tense from the verb in the second part.
a) *If you give* £10 a month, this child *will go* to school.
b) If his family *had* more money, they *would send* him to school.

It is possible to write both types of sentence the other way round.
This child *will go* to school if you *give* . . .
His family *would send* him to school if they *had* . . .

Sentence a suggests that the situation could change and that it is quite possible that the child will go to school.
Sentence b suggests that there is no reason to think the situation will change, we are only imagining what would happen if . . .

2 *Will* is usually abbreviated to *'ll* in spoken English.
He'll have more opportunities if he goes to school.

Would is usually abbreviated to *'d* in spoken English.
If I had more money, *I'd give* £10 a month.

Unit 20

Hopes and plans for the future

1 The following ways of talking about plans and ambitions all take an infinitive:
I'd like to/I want to/I'm going to/I plan to + do

2 *Going to* and *plan to* are used to talk about plans or intentions. *Going to* is used more often than *plan to*.

3 *Want to* and *would like to* are used to talk about events in the future which are seen as desirable but not as fixed plans. *Would like to* is a more polite way of saying *want to*.

Would rather

You can say that someone prefers one situation to another by using *would rather*.
I'd rather stay at home this evening. (than go out)

Tapescripts

I = Interviewer   M = Man   W = Woman   Wa = Waiter   G = Girl

Unit 1

Exercise 2: First languages

Interview A

I Do you speak English at home, Helen?
H No, we speak Chinese. Well, my brothers and sisters and I sometimes speak English but we always speak Chinese to my Mum and Dad.
I Can you read and write Chinese?
H Mmm, not really. I'm learning. I go to Chinese school on Saturday to learn how to read and write Chinese but it's hard. There are over seven thousand characters to learn.

Interview B

I Miguel, what's your first language?
M Spanish. I mean I speak Spanish at home but I think I speak English better than Spanish now. Anyway I can't really write Spanish very well because I learnt to write in English. But I suppose Spanish is really my first language.
I Do your parents speak English?
M No, well, my Dad does, but my Mum doesn't, she can understand a bit, though.

Interview C

I You speak three languages, Ahmed, don't you?
A Yes, my native language is Arabic, and I speak French from when I was at school in Morocco. And English, of course, which I learnt here.
I And can you read and write all these languages?
A Well, I can read and write English because I've been at school here for so long, but I think I write better in Arabic. I think I've forgotten how to write French now.

Exercise 4: Personal information

Interview A

I Your surname's De Luca, isn't it?
A Yes, that's right.
I And you're twenty?
A That's right.
I Where are you from Angela?
A I was born in Lugano, in Switzerland.
I And do you er, still live there?
A Yes, I do.
I Ah, so, you're Swiss?
A No, I was born in Switzerland, but I'm Italian.
I And Italian is your first language.
A That's right.
I Can you speak any other languages besides Italian and English?
A I can speak a little French.
I And German?
A Mmm, not really. We learnt it at school, but I can't really say I can speak it.

Interview B

I Where do you come from, José?
J From Bilbao, in Spain.
I You're Spanish, then.
J Well, really, I'm Basque. Let's say Basque and Spanish.
I And your family name, is that a Basque name?
J Yes, it is. It's Malaxtebarria.
I How do you spell it?
J It's M-A-L-A-X-T-E-B-A-R-R-I-A.
I Thanks, Malaxtebarria. And, er, your age? How old are you?

J Nineteen.

I And what's your first language?

J Basque, but I speak Castilian as well.

I Can you speak any other languages?

J No, I can't.

I What about English?

J Oh, yes, I can speak English, but not fluently.

Exercise 5: Languages people speak

M So, is English the most widely spoken language in the world?

W Well, if we look at the languages that are spoken in the world today, of course Chinese is the most widely spoken because, well, there are so many people in China, over one billion. But the English language is spoken in so many parts of the world now, it's spoken by nearly one billion people as their first or second language. In many parts of Africa for example, people speak fluent English as their language of business or education but they might speak two or three other languages as well. In fact, most Africans speak at least three languages. I suppose that makes them the best linguists in the world, really. And, of course, many schoolchildren in London and New York are pretty good linguists, too. Do you know that 20% of London schoolchildren speak English at school and another language at home? We found about 150 different languages spoken by children in New York schools and 170 languages spoken by London schoolchildren.

M I never knew that.

W It's amazing isn't it? But, you know, one problem with learning English is the vocabulary. The Oxford English Dictionary contains about 500,000 words and they say there are another half a million technical and scientific words that are not yet included in the dictionary.

M Mmm.

W When you think that 2,000 years ago, when Julius Caesar came from Rome to Britain, the English language did not exist.

M Well quite.

W No one in the world spoke English!

Unit 2

Exercise 4: What would you like?

Dialogue A

M1 Right, I'll get these.

M3 Yes, gentlemen?

M1 Erm, a pint of lager for me. Er, how about you, Pete?

M2 Just an orange juice, please. I'm driving.

M3 Ice?

M2 Ice? Uh, . . . yeah, I'll have some ice.

M3 That'll be one pound fifty, please.

M1 Thanks. Er, shall we sit over there?

M2 Fine.

Dialogue B

G1 Oh did he? I don't believe it!

G2 And so I said . . .

Wa Yes, what would you like?

G2 Oh, I don't know. Just let me have a look at the menu. Let me see . . .

G1 Erm. I'll have a cheeseburger, chips and a large coke.

G2 Ugh! I hate cheese. I'll just have a beefburger and chips.

Wa Anything else?

G2 Have you got any orange juice?

Wa Large or small?

G2 Small, please. So anyway, and then I said . . .

Dialogue C

Wa Are you ready to order?

W Er, yes, please. I'll have the roast beef.

Wa Mhm. Would you like a starter?

W No thank . . . oh, why not? I'll have the garlic mushrooms please.

Wa And would you like salad or vegetables with your roast beef?

W Er, what vegetables have you got?

Wa Cauliflower and carrots.

W Er, have you got any cabbage?

Wa No, I'm afraid not.

W Oh, well, never mind, I'll have the carrots.

Wa Carrots. Can I get you anything to drink?

W Er, just a glass of water.

Wa And would you like anything for dessert?

W No thanks.

Exercise 6: Customer calls

Dialogue A

Wa Are you ready to order?

W Er, yes, please. I'll have the roast beef.

Wa Mhm. Would you like a starter?

W No thank . . . oh, why not? I'll have the garlic mushrooms please.

Wa And would you like salad or vegetables with your roast beef?

W Er, what vegetables have you got?

Wa Cauliflower and carrots.

W Er, have you got any cabbage?

Wa No, I'm afraid not.

W Oh, well, never mind, I'll have the carrots.

Wa Carrots. Can I get you anything to drink?

W Er, just a glass of water.

Wa And would you like anything for dessert?

W No thanks.

Dialogue B

W Excuse me?

Wa Yes?

W I'm afraid this bread is stale.

Wa Oh, I'm terribly sorry, I'll get you some fresh, madam.

Unit 3

Exercise 3: I don't believe it!

A No, I think it's a load of rubbish myself. I mean, some people believe anything, don't they? Well, it doesn't make sense, does it, things flying around in the sky, coming down from another planet and all that? No, I think when the scientists say it's happened and we can explain how it happened – I mean, when we have some real proof, then I'll believe it.

B There could be some truth in it, but I tend to think it's just a tourist attraction. I can't explain the photographs. And then there are the photographs of 'Bigfoot', the erm, er, Abominable Snowman in the mountains of India. Well, that's the same sort of thing. I suppose it could be true, but it's the same with all these stories, you'd like to see it for yourself before you believe it.

C Oh, yes. They definitely exist. Yes, I believe that some people come back to haunt us. I mean, we've all had strange feelings about people who are no longer with us, or strange feelings about certain places. I think those feelings are a kind of ghost. We don't always see something, you know, in a long white dress going 'Whooo-ooo' in the middle of the night, but we can have strong feelings about the past. Some people have very strong feelings so they actually begin to see things, something moving, a shape, a light, I don't know. Scientific facts can't explain everything in this world, you know.

Exercise 6: The haunted house

(sound effects)

Unit 4

Exercise 3: What's on?

Interview A

I How long are you in London for?

M Just a few days, I'm afraid.

I Where are you from?

M Sweden.

I And have you enjoyed yourself?

M Oh, I've had a great time. I came to London because of the music. Erm, I've been to . . . I don't know how many clubs. They were great, especially the Latin jazz clubs, they were absolutely fantastic. Well, except for one. It was really boring. There were only about five or six people there so there was no atmosphere. But apart from that I've enjoyed them all.

I And what are your plans for the rest of the holiday?

M Well, I'm going to visit a few more jazz clubs and then that's it. I'm going to leave on Monday. Then it's back to work, I'm afraid.

Interview B

I So you're over from the States?

W That's right. We've been here about er, two and a half weeks and we've got another three days before we go back.

I Have you been to the theatre here?

W Oh, yes. Theatre, opera, concerts, the lot. We've seen some magnificent things at the theatre, really excellent – the acting, the stage sets, the whole atmosphere, really, it was fantastic.

I Which do you think was your favourite play?

W It's hard to say. Er, the Shakespeare play, that was brilliant, and then we saw a comedy last night, that was really funny, I loved that. I don't know, it's been a very entertaining two weeks, I think I've enjoyed most things I've seen.

I And what's next, then?

W The bank! Tomorrow morning I'm going to cash some more traveller's cheques. You can spend quite a lot of money in London, you know. Never mind, it's been worth it. The most entertaining two weeks I've had for a long time. And I think I'll come back next year if I can. If I have enough money left that is!

Interview C

I Could you tell me where you're from?

W From Italy, Milan.

I And how long are you going to be in London?

W For another year. I'm working here at the moment.

I Do you go out much to theatres and concerts and so on?

W Oh, I do. But not as often as I'd like to. I love opera and most kinds of music, in fact. I've been to quite a lot of concerts in the last two or three weeks.

I Classical concerts?

W Yes, mostly. I'm going to go to a couple of concerts this weekend, at the Royal Festival Hall.

I And what about opera?

W Oh, I love opera but I went to see a Verdi opera last month and I didn't like it at all. It was really dreadful. Maybe it's because I prefer Italian opera sung in Italian, not English, I don't know. Anyway I thought it sounded awful. But I'll try another English opera again in a few weeks.

I What about the next few days? You've got the concert at the weekend, and then?

W Then I'm going to take it easy for a few days. I think you can do too much.

Unit 5

Exercise 3: Have you ever lived abroad?

I Have you ever lived abroad, Phyllis?

P Yes, I have actually. What about you?

I No, unfortunately I haven't.

P Oh, what a shame!

I Where did you live when you were abroad?

P I lived in Australia.

I Really? That's a long way away.

P Mhm, mhm, yes!

I How long were you there for?

P I was there for twelve years.

I Oh! What a long time!

P Yes, it is rather.

I Erm, so how long have you been back in the UK?

P I've been back about erm, ten years now.

I Mhm, mhm. When you were in Australia, did you think of it as your home?

P Well, it depends on what you mean by home. When I was . . . home to me is being near the people you're fond of.

I Mhm, mhm, yeah. So does that mean that your family were with you in Australia?

P Yes, they were there with me.

I And presumably they've . . . they came back to the UK?

P Yes, they did. They came back with me.

I Mhm, mhm. Erm, if you had a choice, where do you think you'd be living now?

P Oh, I would really like to go back to Australia.

I Oh, yeah? Why's that?

P Well, for one thing, it's the climate –

I Mhm.

P – and, er, secondly, it's . . . very relaxed.

I Oh? In what way?

P Well, you know, the way of life, nobody hurries.

I Mhm. Is that at work as well as socially?

P That's right, everything.

Unit 6

Exercise 2: Women's work?

I Careers officers around the country are reporting that more women are applying for jobs which have traditionally been held by men. This morning I am speaking to Jane Richards, a schools careers officer based in London. Good morning, Jane.

J Good morning.

I Jane, are you finding that women's career choices are changing?

J Yes, I am.

I And why do you think that's happening?

J Well, there are many reasons. One very important one is the media, radio and television. Girls see a popular young actress playing a car mechanic, for example, and this makes them think – well, why not? Why couldn't I become a car mechanic, or a plumber, or an electrician? Erm, another reason is that careers officers, like myself are trying very hard to make both sexes aware of all the job options, including the non-traditional ones.

I And what do you mean by non-traditional?

J Well, non-traditional job choices for women, for example, would be things like plumbing and car mechanics. For men, housekeeping would be quite a non-traditional career choice.

I Yes, I see. But er, isn't it true that most girls still choose stereotyped jobs? For example, a survey of Scottish school-leavers showed that 75% of girls still choose traditional women's jobs like nursing, clerical work or working in shops.

J Yes, that's true, and of course I'm not saying that things are changing overnight. But they are changing.

I Why is it so important, do you think, that people change their attitudes?

J Because, at the moment, there are fewer and fewer children leaving school in Britain. This means that we're going to need women more and more in the work force. But women are not going to be qualified unless attitudes – both men's and women's – change dramatically. At the moment, the change isn't big or fast enough, and in some cases Britain is seriously lagging behind other countries . . .

Unit 7

Exercise 2: The great outdoors

A To do it properly, you have to go far away from everyday conveniences such as hot water, telephones, restaurants and other mod cons like that. It's because it's so different from normal everyday life, I mean, I really enjoy relaxing, eating and sleeping in the middle of mountains or forests. Do you know, I can still remember my first night out there on my own. I loved waking up in the early hours of the morning and seeing this clear sky full of shooting stars. I remember, I jumped up and ran down to this freezing cold river for a wash. And, I mean, normally, at home, I hate getting up in the morning, but out there it's something different.

B I don't know, it's hard to explain the feeling. It isn't really like flying, it's like dreaming that you're flying. One minute your feet are running on the hillside and the next minute you're hanging in the air. I mean, it isn't like being in water or walking on the moon, it's a special sensation. Really wonderful. But during my first lesson at the centre I spent most of my time watching everyone else and I was quite scared of doing it myself. In fact, I really wasn't looking forward to the moment when my feet left the

ground. But when I finally did it I felt like telling the world how fantastic it was.

C You know, it's very popular in France – it's been popular over there for the last ten years, in fact. Well, I decided to try because I was good at rock climbing but I wanted to do something different, more challenging, if you know what I mean. I suppose it is dangerous but when you're out there you feel like you're completely alone, you know, it's, it's almost like being at the edge of the world. I'd like to go to Canada and try over there now. There are waterfalls in the Canadian Rockies that are 300 metres high – can you imagine? I suppose sometimes I am scared of falling but that doesn't stop me. Maybe it's exciting because it's so dangerous. Anyway I can't stand just sitting about doing nothing.

Unit 8

Exercise 2: How we used to look

I So how long have you been a fashion editor now?

W Let's see, it was about 1970 when I started.

I So, you've seen lots of different fashions come and go, I suppose.

W Oh, yes. When I first came, in the early seventies, it was all flared trousers, you know, tight at the top and wide at the bottom and long skirts for women.

I Yes.

W And they used to wear lots of jewellery – beads, necklaces, earrings . . . and lots of Indian clothes. You know, the hippie look really. Of course, that's when both men and women used to have really long hair, you remember?

I Yes, I do. I think they used to look quite romantic in those days. I wouldn't like to wear those kind of clothes now, though. But before that they didn't use to have all those long clothes and long hair, did they?

W No, well, at least, the men didn't use to have long hair, and in the nineteen sixties, it used to be fashionable for women to have very short skirts – mini-skirts – big black eyes, you know, and lots of make up.

I So how did men use to look in the sixties?

W Well, dark sunglasses used to be very popular and they used to have their hair in a long fringe at the front. And of course, curly hair was out.

I Oh?

W Everyone used to try and get their hair straight. Sometimes girls even ironed their hair. But really, the start of teenage fashion was in the fifties with Rock 'n' Roll –

I Right.

W – men in big suede shoes, jeans and T-shirts and all that greasy hair. I always think the women used to look much better than the men with their pony tails and big full skirts – great for dancing.

I Yes, I've seen photos of my Mum and Dad like that. They look really funny. But what about more recently?

W Well, the late seventies was the start of the Punk era – spiky hair, long boots, tight black trousers with lots of chains and, of course, the face became very important again. Both men and women used to put on lots of face make-up in different colours. And then the eighties was the sporty decade, I suppose – people looking as if they were going running or cycling. When you look back, yes, I suppose people did use to look funny but fashion's always like that, isn't it? You know, when you see how we used to look.

Exercise 6: Biography

. . . And thanks very much for all your questions. Now before we finish tonight's show I'll just tell you about next week's guest on the phone-in. Get your questions ready for the beautiful and talented Yazz. Yazz is going to be talking about her past, how she used to be a fashion model in Germany before she made it in the world of music. And how, in her younger days, she used to play volleyball for the under-19s England volleyball team. At school, apparently, she was excellent at sport and in fact she still is very interested in keeping fit and works out in the gym twice a week and cycles every day. So you could see her cycling to the studio next week. Yazz tells me she thinks health is very important and as well as plenty of exercise she has a very particular macrobiotic diet which means lots of rice, beans and seaweed. But no meat and dairy produce for Yazz. Well, it seems to keep her looking good. Born Yasmin Evans, under the sign of Taurus the bull on the 19th May 1963 to a Jamaican father and a Scottish mother. But interestingly, it's not Scotland or Jamaica that's her favourite country – it's Italy. She says Italy is a beautiful and exciting place. So for the equally beautiful and exciting Yazz, tune in same time, same place, next week. Take care.

Unit 9

Exercise 2: The poison-arrow frog

Part 1

I Good morning. And in our studio today we have Jayne Gray who has just finished writing an unusual book on frogs. Jayne, how did you become interested in frogs in the first place?

J Well, when I was a child we had lots of frogs in the garden and I used to spend hours watching them and I guess it just grew from there.

I I see. In your book, you give lots of unusual and surprising facts about frogs. You mention one in particular called the poison-arrow frog. It certainly has an unusual name.

J Yes, it does. In fact, the poison-arrow frog actually got its name because the Colombian Indians used to put its poison on their arrows.

I Really? did they?

J Yes, the poison is incredibly deadly. It's so strong, in fact, that if just .00001 of a gram of it gets into your blood, you'll die.

I Really? That is deadly.

Part 2

I How big are these frogs? Are they quite large?

J Not at all. They're very small, in fact. They range in size from 1.5 to 5 cm. But they're usually quite colourful. As you can see, the one in the photograph is bright orange. Their bright bodies are actually a warning to other animals. In fact, I think they're very pretty.

I Yes, I suppose so, but that's not to say that I'd like to find one in my garden.

J Oh, you wouldn't. Poison-arrow frogs live in the tropical areas of America. They often live close to streams. And although most of them live on the forest floor, one species actually lives in the treetops. So you see, you're quite safe.

I Well, that's a relief! Now in your book you also mention . . .

Unit 10

Exercise 4: Visitors to London

M Hi! Phew! Sorry I'm late. Have you been waiting long?

W No, I've just arrived, actually. I've been shopping for presents. I think I've bought them all now.

M Good. Ugh! I suppose this must be typically English weather.

W I suppose so. It's been raining all morning.

M Yeah!

W Anyway, what about you? What have you been doing?

M Me? Oh, I've been writing postcards all morning. I think I've written them all now.

W Good. Where shall we go now then?

M Well, let's see, we've seen St Paul's Cathedral, Westminster Abbey, Big Ben. Ah! We haven't been to the Tower of London yet.

W Well, the Tower of London's fine with me. Oh, look. There's a taxi!

M Taxi!

Exercise 5: The Tower of London

Good morning ladies and gentlemen. This morning we'll be going round the Tower of London, which was first built by William the Conqueror in the eleventh century for the purpose of protecting and controlling the City of London. Including the moat, which is now dry, the Tower covers an area of 18 acres. Over the years, the Tower has been used as a fortress, a palace and a prison.

It was occupied as a palace by all the Kings and Queens of England down to James I. The custom was for each king or queen to stay in the Tower the night before he or she was crowned and to ride from the Tower, through the City, to Westminster.

Of course, the Tower is also famous because it has always guarded the Crown Jewels and every year millions of tourists visit the Tower to observe these rare and priceless gems.

On the right now is St Thomas's Tower, with the Traitors' Gate beneath. When the Thames was more of a highway than it is at present, this gate was often used as an entrance to the Tower. In later times, it was used as a landing place for prisoners, who passed under the arch on their way to prison or to be executed. Here many famous prisoners, including Queen Anne Boleyn, second wife of King Henry VIII, Sir Thomas Moore, Queen Katharine Howard . . .

Unit 11

Exercise 2: Breaking the habit

I First of all, Dr Richards, can you explain what you mean when you use the word chocoholic?

Dr Yes. By chocoholic I mean someone who is addicted to chocolate.

I Ah! Well, we all know chocolate tastes very nice, but can you actually become addicted to it?

Dr Oh, yes. Chocolate contains chemicals which are quite addictive. It's, it's a much more common problem than you think. Last year people in Britain spent over £2.3 billion on chocolate. That's a lot of chocolate.

I It certainly is. So erm, what advice do you have for chocoholics who want to give up?

Dr Well, the most important thing is to cut down gradually, rather than try to give up all at once.

I Why's that?

Dr Because it could lead to bingeing, that's to say you could give up completely for 3 days, then go out and eat a whole packet of chocolate biscuits at once.

I I see.

Dr First, you should keep a diary for 10 days. Find out when you eat the most chocolate and how you are feeling when you eat it. Next you should set yourself a weekly plan. If you eat 15 bars of chocolate a week, cut down to 12 in the first week, 10 in the second and so on. And have plenty of fresh fruit available as an alternative to chocolate. Finally when you have achieved your goal, treat yourself! Buy a few magazines or, or go to the cinema with the money you've saved.

I Well, thank you very much, Dr Richards.

TAPESCRIPTS

Exercise 5: I'd rather you didn't

M It's great to see you! Do you mind if I sit down?

W Well, actually . . .

M Thanks. How are you? I haven't seen you for ages!

W Fine thanks. And you?

M Oh, great. You don't mind if I smoke, do you?

W Well, actually, I'd rather you didn't.

M Oh well . . . Oh, I see you've finished your drink. Can I get you another one?

W No, thank you very much. In fact, erm . . . oh dear! Is that the time? I'm afraid I really must be going.

M Oh what a shame! Maybe we could go for dinner sometime soon? Are you free on Friday?

W I'm afraid not. I've arranged to go to the theatre with some friends.

M Oh, maybe some other time then.

W Yes, I'll give you a ring sometime.

Unit 12

Exercise 2: Who says what?

Mark: It's a means of buying what I want. Money doesn't mean any thing to me. It's just a piece of paper, and until it's actually changed to something, like a machine, or a car, it's useless – something you put away in a bank. And money sitting in a bank is no use to anyone.

Paul: It doesn't mean a great lot. It used to be important – when I was married. But now I'm not. I've only got myself to think about, so I don't worry about it. As long as I've got enough to eat, and to have a few drinks at night, that's it, I'm happy, I don't want anything else.

Mrs Cooper: In business, money means profits. If a business doesn't produce profits, then it won't be able to exist, because any business well, we measure success by the profits we make. An artist may measure success by something else, a craftsman by something else, but our business is to make money.

Exercise 5: At the Bank

Yen, French francs, pesetas, Swiss francs, dollar, lira, Hong Kong dollar, pound sterling, Deutschmark.

Unit 13

Exercise 5: What's the matter?

Dialogue A

W1 Oh, Jane! What happened?

W2 I had an accident on my bike. A car ran into me.

W1 Oh no! That's awful. How badly injured are you?

W2 Oh, not too bad. I've got a broken ankle and a sore back. That's all.

W1 Well, don't you think you'd better stay at home and take it easy for a few days?

W2 No, I'm all right, really.

Dialogue B

M1 Is something the matter?

M2 Mhm. I feel sick and I've got a terrible headache.

M1 Well, it serves you right for staying out so late.

M2 Mhm.

M1 You should stop all these late nights and get to bed early for a change.

M2 OK, OK, I will.

Dialogue C

M1 What's wrong? You look terrible!

M2 Yeah, I've just cut my finger on this blade.

M1 Oh, let's have a look. That looks quite serious, you'd better get a few stitches in that. Come on I think we should take you to the hospital.

M2 Yes, maybe you're right.

Exercise 6: Food for thought

Part 1

I Sue, I believe the story of the disease, Kuru, is famous in medical history?

S Oh, yes. I think most medical students have read about Kuru at some time or other.

I And it was just one tribe of cannibals who used to get this disease, wasn't it?

S Yes, that's right. It was the Fore Tribe of Papua New Guinea. They used to eat the bodies of the dead of the tribe. And they particularly liked the brains of the dead person because they thought that all the knowledge of the tribe's history was in a person's brain. By eating the brain they would remember their past and keep the knowledge.

I I see. Not a bad idea, really, is it?

S Well, you can see why the Fore Tribe didn't want to give up their practice of cannibalism. I mean, this was in the 1950s and there weren't many cannibal tribes left in the world. The government of Papua New Guinea had banned cannibalism several years before. But for these people it was a very important custom. It wasn't because they had no other food – it was part of their history.

I But it caused serious problems, didn't it?

S Yes, unfortunately many members of the Fore Tribe used to get this strange disease called Kuru, which was a terrible disease of the brain.

I And what were the symptoms of Kuru exactly?

S Well, people with Kuru would begin to act in strange ways, for example, they used to laugh for no reason and er, they lost their memory and then they used to walk in a funny way. A bit like someone who was drunk. After a time, they lost the ability to speak and then finally they couldn't move at all. And then they died. A terrible disease.

I Yes, awful. And it was the women who got it much more than the men.

S Yes, that's right. Well, they used to prepare the food you see.

Part 2

I I'm not sure what you mean, about the women preparing the food.

S Oh, well. You know with any meat which is diseased you can catch the disease much more easily when the meat is raw – before it's cooked. So, the women prepared the food and they would try little bits before it was cooked properly and it was on their fingers and so on.

I Oh, right. So the disease was passed on by eating the brain of someone who had died from Kuru. And the cooked meat was less dangerous than raw meat.

S Exactly. Of course scientists had studied the tribe for many years before they discovered the cause of the disease.

I And then did they stop, you know, practising cannibalism?

S Oh, yes. But only after the scientists had explained why it was so dangerous.

I And now?

S Oh, no one has had Kuru for many years now.

I A happy ending?

S Yes, I think that's why medical scientists like the story so much. They found the perfect cure!

Unit 14

Exercise 2: Police advice

Good afternoon, and welcome to England. We hope that your visit here will be a pleasant one. Today, I would like to draw your attention to a few of our laws and other matters which may concern you.

The first one concerns drinking. Now, you may not buy alcohol in this country if you are under 18 years of age, nor may your friends buy it for you – that is also against the law.

Secondly, noise. Enjoy yourselves by all means, but erm, please don't make unnecessary noise, particularly at night. We ask you to respect other people who may wish to be quiet.

Thirdly, crossing the road. Beware. The traffic moves on the left side of the road in this country, so be careful. Use pedestrian crossings and do not take any chances when crossing the road.

My next point concerns litter. It is an offence to drop litter in the street. When you have something to throw away, please put it in your pocket and take it home, or put it in a litter bin.

Finally, as regards smoking, it is illegal to buy cigarettes or tobacco if you are under 16 years of age.

I'd like to finish by saying that if you require any sort of help or assistance, you should contact your local police station, who will be pleased to help you.

Now, are there any questions?

Unit 15

Exercise 2: The blue whale

I Anne, you're interested in, well, in all wild-life, but I know you have a special interest in whales.

A Yes, that's right. To me, whales are such magnificent animals.

I But you're afraid they're in danger of becoming extinct.

A I'm afraid that's true. They've been around for 50 million years now but I think we're seeing their last few years on earth.

I And this is because so many are killed each year for different kinds of products?

A Yes, and in many cases this is quite unnecessary.

I Which products exactly?

A Oh, the list is endless. Er, well, let's take whale oil. That's used in soaps, margarine, cosmetics, erm, in such things as drum skins, tennis racket strings and shoe laces, even in photographic film and anti-freeze for cars. And its meat is used in pet food. To think the meat of this wonderful and dying animal is given to our cats and dogs. I mean, I find that a tragedy.

I Mhm.

A And, of course, some jewellery, like er, earrings and necklaces are made from its bones. If you look at some expensive pipes and cigarette holders you'll find some of them are made from whale bone, too. You don't find it so much these days but we used to make piano keys, umbrellas – and, of course, lots of ladies' underwear was made from whale bone in the past. Very sad.

I And I believe one of the whales in very great danger is the blue whale?

A Yes. About a third of a million blue whales have been killed this century, although they have been protected by law since 1966.

I This is the biggest whale, isn't it?

A That's right. It's an enormous creature. The male is usually about 25 metres long, and weighs about 140 tonnes.

I Goodness! I can't imagine how much 140 tonnes is!

A Well, that's about as much as 2,000 people would weigh.

I 2,000! That's amazing!

A Oh, it is an amazing creature. Just to give you another idea, its tongue weighs about the same as a small elephant and it has three stomachs. In the summer it eats about 4% of its bodyweight in food per day, that's about 5 tonnes of food per day.

I 5 tonnes?

A Yes, that's enough to feed about, oh, three thousand

people! Well it needs to eat that much because in the winter, it lives for about 8 months without any food at all. There are so many incredible facts about this animal. For instance, it lives to around 35 years old, it can swim at up to 50km/h if it's being chased, it has a brain four times as big as a man's, and makes a low humming sound that can be detected up to 160 km away . . .

Exercise 5: Are you an animal lover?

Dialogue A

W Well, as far as I'm concerned, we shouldn't kill animals at all.

M What, never?

W No. We don't need to eat animal flesh. There are plenty of things to eat instead of meat and fish.

M Mhm. Yes, I suppose that's true.

W Yeah, and, quite frankly, I think we should stop selling all meat and fish foods completely. Everyone'd be a lot healthier.

M Oh, I don't know about that, that's a bit extreme isn't it?

Dialogue B

W1 I think it's disgusting people wearing hats and coats like that.

W2 Yes, I agree.

W1 I mean, just think of all the animals they have to kill to make one fur coat.

W2 That's right. But some people don't care about it.

W1 Mhm, quite honestly, I don't think we should buy any leather goods either. It's just the same thing. We could easily make shoes and bags and whatever out of plastic.

W2 Well, I'm not sure I agree with you there.

W1 But I mean, it's still using animals for something that's not really necessary.

W2 Mhm. I suppose you've got a point.

Unit 16

Exercise 2: A good match

(Sound effects)

Exercise 3: Talking to a professional

I Dave, you're one of Britain's top champions now. When did you start?

D Well, I'm eighteen now and I came into the sport from cycling. I've been doing it for about three years now, I suppose.

I And were you good at it from the start?

D No, not really. It took me a couple of years to reach a good standard. And I've been a professional for about a year now.

I How hard do you have to train?

D I try to train for about six hours every day. Erm, you have to spend a lot of time on it but my girlfriend trains with me so we can have a lot of fun training

together. It's a pity but it, it's much more popular with boys than girls, although girls are beginning to get more interested.

I Which countries take part in competitions?

D America is still the top place. After that England's the next best place. And it's also very popular in Spain and Germany. I've been to Europe to compete and er, I'm going to the States this year.

I Any advice for youngsters interested in the sport?

D Erm, I think 12 is the best age to start. I suggest you get a good quality board plus some protective gear, like a good helmet – and then, well, just practise as much as possible. You'll probably find it difficult to balance at first, but you'll soon get more confident.

I It's not expensive to get going, is it?

D No. All you need at first is the board and an open space on hard ground. When you've learned how to stand on the board and can do simple turns you can try building up a bit of speed. Erm, I suppose it's a bit like skiing or skating – er, the better you are the more exciting it is. But, you know, I'd like to see more TV coverage. You can see it occasionally on TV but I'd like to see it on TV three or four times a week. I mean, it's so popular now with young people.

I Well, thanks a lot, Dave. And all the best in the States this year.

D Thank you.

Exercise 6: Love it or hate it

A: Me, no. I don't do any sport now. I'm over forty and not very fit. I'd like to do some sport again, but I don't have time these days.

B: I do like sport, and I enjoy a game of badminton occasionally, but I'm not that keen – I just go along with my friends and have an evening out.

C: I'm still at school and we have to do sport once a week. I try to miss it if I can. I've never seen a game of football in my life, for example, and I don't think I ever will. I feel the same way about all sport.

D: I think I'll always do some kind of sport. For instance, I'm going skiing this year. I'm not really any good, but I've always been interested in sport. I just enjoy it.

E: Sport is the greatest activity of all. I think if you're not interested in sport, you're not interested in life. Sport is what makes us different from animals.

Unit 17

Exercise 2: I hated school

I I hear you weren't very keen on school, Chris?

C No, I hated it. Awful place.

I Why did you dislike it so much?

C I suppose, well, I'd grown up in West Africa, in Sierra

Leone, and erm, out there, as a kid, you were really free, and my parents were working out there, you see. Erm, my Mum was a primary school teacher and she'd taught me everything till I was about nine and then I suppose they thought I'd better go to school. So I came here and started school on my ninth birthday. I can still remember the shock of being in the middle of West Africa one minute and then suddenly being in a strange place with about 500 other white kids who I'd never seen before.

I Mhm.

C And I wasn't used to all these dos and don'ts. You know, don't use this door, use that door, don't go up these stairs – all that kind of thing. I couldn't understand it. So, er, I used to break the rules whenever I could and I was always in trouble with the teachers.

I So what was the typical day like?

C Oh, everything was controlled by bells. In the morning a bell would ring and then we all had to get up about half past seven and get ready for breakfast. After breakfast, another bell so we had to come back to the dormitories to make sure all the beds were made etc. Erm, then lessons all day. And in the evening we had to do, oh, two hours of homework. The teachers used to walk round to make sure we were working. Then we had about, about an hour's free time before we had to go to bed. Lights-out was at 10 pm and we weren't allowed to talk after that.

I What about meals?

C Oh, mealtimes. Yeah, that was another story. Every mealtime was the same. We had to queue outside the dining room until the teachers let us in. And then we all had to wait behind our chairs until the teachers told us to sit down. We weren't allowed to speak until the meal started.

I Really?

C Oh, yes. And then, of course, you weren't allowed out of the school without permission. If you went out you had to write on a piece of paper where you were going, how long you were staying etc. The older boys were allowed out on Saturdays and Sundays, and they didn't have to get special permission but erm, they had to be back before eleven at night.

I This was the boys of about 16 or 17, right?

C Yeah.

I And the boys all slept in a big dormitory?

C Yes, fifty of us.

I Fifteen?

C No, fifty.

I Fifty?

C That's right. 25 on one side, 25 on the other. We had to leave the windows open at night for fresh air. As you can probably imagine, with 50 boys in one room

it can get pretty stuffy.

I I should think so. And what about now? Would you send your own children to boarding school?

C No, I don't think I could. Oh, I suppose they're different now, – and then, well, I hated it but I still feel it's good in some ways. It teaches you to be independent, for example. But erm, no, I don't think I'd send my children to boarding school. Not one like mine, anyway.

Unit 18

Exercise 3: Will anything stay the same?

I In our studio this morning we have author Jeremy Lane. He believes that the next ten years will be a time of rapid progress isn't that right, Mr Lane?

J.L Yes, that's right. In fact, I think we'll see some pretty amazing changes in the next ten years in just about every area of life.

I Can you give some examples of the sort of changes you expect to see?

J.L Yes. Health care will improve. In fact, scientists may finally find a cure for cancer in the next ten years, and vaccines for diseases like Aids and the common cold. One thing is certain – everyone will be living much longer.

I That's good news. What about leisure? Will we have more time for that?

J.L Oh yes. We'll have much more free time. By the year 2000, we'll be working an average of just 35 hours a week and we'll have 15 weeks holiday. In fact, we'll probably take two or three holidays a year. People may spend their holiday time in France, Spain or Italy. Or they may spend it further away in places like Africa, America and the Far East. Air travel will be cheaper, so destinations that are further away will be more popular.

I I see. Tell me. Will anything stay the same?

J.L Oh yes, well one thing anyway. There'll be lots of new places to go to, but the sun will still be people's biggest reason for going away. Whatever happens, people will still want to come back from holiday with a nice suntan.

Unit 19

Exercise 6: The wealth in the world

I And there is, of course, a big difference between the very rich and the very poor.

M Oh, yes, indeed. Er, if, for example, you look at three of the richest countries in the world – er, Qatar, the United Arab Emirates and Bermuda – er, they all have an average annual income per person of over £20,000. Then compare these countries with, say, Bangladesh with an average annual income of £100 or Chad, in

Central Africa, with about £60. Well, you can see the enormous difference between some of the richest and some of the poorest countries.

I But you can compare other things as well as actual money, can't you?

M Yes, you can. Er, if you look at car ownership, for example, you see that about 500 out of every 1,000 people in the USA own cars.

I About 50%.

M That's right. But only about one person in every 1,000 owns a car in India. And then, for example, people in richer countries generally expect to have running water in their homes but only 10% of homes in Afghanistan and Ethiopia have running water and only 18% of homes in Pakistan and Paraguay have electricity. Wealth and poverty is not just a question of money.

I And then, most of the wealth in the world is owned by a small number of people, isn't it?

M Oh, yes. About 90% of the world's population lives on less than half of the total wealth in the world.

I And what about the very rich? Can you give us an example of how much wealth some people have?

M Well, er, one example of a very wealthy man is the musician and songwriter, Paul McCartney. He earns about £25 million a year, that's about £45 a minute or £70,000 a day.

I That's an amazing amount of money. In fact, every two minutes, he can earn the same amount as some people in the world earn in a year!

M That's right. But I have to say, er, one fact that I always find quite shocking is how much money people spend on their pets. Here in Britain, we spend an average of £2 billion a year on our pets and that money goes mainly on food for cats and dogs. £2 billion is an awful lot of money for some countries.

Unit 20

Exercise 4: I'd really like to . . .

Interview A

I Richard, you've just left school, haven't you?

R Yes, last month.

I So, what now? What do you plan to do next?

R Well, I've thought about university. I'm really interested in design. I'd like to get a job with a design company but I'm going to do a one-year course in design first. I'm starting next month, in fact. Then next year I'm going to try to find a job and go on studying part-time.

I What about marriage? Girlfriends? Any plans there?

R No, well definitely not marriage, not yet. I'll probably get married one day, but I want to start my career and earn some money before I start thinking about that.

I And you're going to carry on living with your parents for the moment?

R Yes, I'm going to live at home until I save a bit of money. I'd like to have my own place you know, but well, I get on OK with my Mum and Dad and lots of my friends are still around here, so I don't plan to move just yet. Maybe I'm just lazy!

Interview B

I Nicole, you've been working as an au-pair here, haven't you?

N Yes, for just over a year now.

I Are you going to stay much longer?

N Well, a few more months, but erm, then I'm definitely going to go back to France at the end of the year. I've got to finish my degree. I know I'll find it hard at first, going back to studying, but I can't stay here forever.

I Do you think you'll come back?

N Oh, I hope so! But if I work abroad again I am going to try to get a job in Spain. I'd really like to learn Spanish now.

I Do you think you'll forget the English you've learned?

N Well, maybe a bit, but I'm going to do some courses in English when I get back to France. And I've got lots of tapes of radio and TV programmes and books in English so I'm going to carry on practising English there.

I Is your university degree in English?

N No, electronics, but I think the English I've learned will help me a lot.

I Well, good luck.

N Thank you.

Addison Wesley Longman Limited
Edinburgh Gate, Harlow,
Essex CM20 2JE, England
and Associated Companies throughout the world.

© Nelson ELT 1992

First published by Collin ELT 1991
This edition published by Addison Wesley Longman Ltd. 1996

Fourth impression 1997

ISBN 0-17-556621-6

Produced by Longman Asia Limited, Hong Kong.
EPC/04

Acknowledgements

The publishers are grateful to the following for permission to reproduce the
copyright material on the pages indicated.

Airtours Plc for Carousel text (page 50); extract from *The Boomerang Book* by
Benjamin Ruhe, Eric Darnell and Campbell Morris, reproduced by kind
permission of Angus & Roberton (UK) (page 47); the Automobile Association
for Maxim Chinese, Tuttons and The Stockpot, from the *AA Best Value in
Britain Guide 1988* (page 3); **Best** magazine for "There's no easy way down the
Himalayas" (page 56) and "The lair of the dog" (page 60); Grace Jones text
(pages 16, 48) interview by Jim Shelley, and Katherine Hamnett text (page 48)
interview by Paul Mathur both from **Blitz** magazine, November 1989.
Reproduced by kind permission of the publishers. © Jigsaw Publications Ltd;
Bodypower magazine Vol 8, no 9, September 1989 for "Superfit" from Bev
Hahn article (page 25); Janet and Colin Bord for material from *Mysterious
Britain* published by Grafton Books (page 5); "The Tower of London" (page
72) reproduced with the permission of the Controller of Her Majesty's
Stationery Office; **The Evening Standard** for "World Cup Drama" (page 32);
Express Newspapers Plc for "Women at work" (pages 12, 70) from "Kylie
steers the girls to new careers"; Guinness Publishing Limited 1990 for "the
tallest man", "the heaviest woman", "the hottest place" (all page 18) and "TV
watching" (page 7) © Guinness Publishing Limited 1990; "The least successful
nurse" (page 49), excerpt from *The Return of Heroic Failures* (US title:
Cannibals in the Cafeteria and Other Fabulous Failures) by Stephen Pile.
Copyright © 1988 by Stephen Pile. Reprinted by permission of Harper & Row,
Publishers, inc.; Horniman Museum for text (page 55); **Outdoor Action**, 13
Park House, 140 Battersea Park Rd, London, SW11 4NB, September 1989
issue, for "Flying Start" by Catherine Moore and "Freestyle" by Paul Traynor
(tapescripts A and B page 70); Oxford University Press for "Where's home?"
(page 10) from Choices © Oxford University Press 1985, by Jean Mills and Les
Stringer; **Plan International** - World Family for texts on Suresh and Suhartono
(pages 37, 59); **Resurgence Ltd** for "Small Schools" (page 34) from
"Cooleenbridge" and "Danish Model", Resurgence 130; World's Children - the
magazine of **Save the Children**, December 1987, for text (page 60) from "New
Horizons for Babli"; "The least successful nurse" (page 49) reprinted by
permission of Secker and Warburg Limited; "The safer sex" (page12), "We love
you British" (page 19), "Stop smoking or I'll bring down the jet" (page 21),
"Student with a £30,000 plan" (page 23), "We wanna earn £30,000 by 30 say
Tycoon Teens" (page 39), "9,500 flee homes as forest fires spread " (page 45),
"Mt Blanc cut down to size" (page 49), "Property boss gives £48 million to
poor" (page 52), Breaking the habit (page 72) from "Gentle cuts will quell the
craving", all reproduced by kind permission of **Today** newspaper; "the fastest
growing city", "the largest town", "the cheapest city", "the longest name" (all
page 17), "the longest underground", "the most expensive film", "the most
successful group", (all page 18), "rich and poor countries" (page 38), "privately
owned cars", "water in our homes", "world incomes", "electricity at home" and
"golden Beatle" (all page 38 and tapescript page 76), "crowded countries", and
"the emptiest countries" (page 49), "different money" (page 52), all reproduced
from *Countries of the World Facts* by permission of Usborne Publishing Ltd
London; "wolf children", "apeman", "apeman's hands" (page 29), "fastest
mammal", "largest mammal", "most dangerous bat" (page 55), all reproduced
from *Mysteries and Marvels of the Animal World* by permission of Usborne
Publishing Limited, London.

The publishers would also like to thank Dr Tony Martin of the Cambridge Sea
Mammal Research Unit for his help with the facts about the blue whale.

Photographs

Bryan and Cherry Alexander (page 9); All-Sport Photographic Ltd (pages 13,
31, x 2, 32); Dean Brewis/Bodypower Magazine (page 25); Stuart Boreham
(pages 12, 23, 39, 40 x 2); Cephas Picture Library (page 38 x 2); Trevor
Clifford with art direction by Sandie Huskinson-Rolfe (Photoseekers) (page 21);
Bruce Coleman Ltd (pages17, 29); Colorsport (pages 31 x 2, 32 x 2);
Compix/John Leach (page 26); Fortean Picture Library (page 5); Gordon
Gadsby (page 13); Sally and Richard Greenhill (pages 9, 33); Susan Griggs
Agency Ltd (page 12); Hamleys, London (page 38); Mark Harrison (page 7,
21); The Hulton Picture Company (page 15); The Image Bank (pages 9, 13, 20
x 3, 31, 33 x 2); Images Colour Library Ltd (page 20); John Launois/Black
Star/Colorific! (page 9); Magnum Photos Ltd (page 37); The Natural History
Museum (page 29); Nursing Standard (page 11); Christine Pemberton/The
Hutchison Library Ltd (page 37); Pictorial Press Ltd (page15); PLAN
International (page 37 x 2); Rex Features Ltd (pages 15, 16 x 2); David
Scammel (page 13); Chris Schwarz/Aspect Picture Library (page 37); Martin
Shallcross (pages 1, 31); Southdown Press/Solo (page 11); Frank Spooner
Pictures (page 8 x 3); Times Newspapers Ltd (page 24); Tropix Photographic
Library (page 10); Vintage Magazine Picture Library (page 15); Weight
Watchers Magazine (page 26).

Illustrations

Alan Austin (pages 42, 43, 49, 51, 53, 54, 58, 60); Jane Brewster (pages 6, 42,
45, 46, 47, 51); Peter Bull (pages 17, 29); Adam Everard (pages 23, 24, 34, 36);
David Harding (pages 11, 27, 37, 38); Mark Harrison (page 7); Robin
Heighway-Bury (pages 3, 4, 19, 21); Graham Humphreys (pages 5, 6); Stephen
Jeffrey (pages 1, 2, 25, 26); Jonno (pages 3, 4, 8, 10, 12, 13, 21, 22, 24, 28, 30,
40, 46); Sarah Perkins (pages 15, 16, 29, 30, 39); Lynne Robertson (pages 9,
18); Danny Staples (page 55); all airbrush work by Illustrated Arts.

The publishers have made every effort to contact owners of
copyright. They apologise for any omissions, and if details are sent,
will be glad to rectify these when the title is reprinted.

Design: Gregor Arthur

The authors wish to express their gratitude to the editors:
Gabby Pritchard, Clare Leeds, Judith Cunningham and Brigit Viney
and also to the following for their help:
Martin Mulloy, Christopher Wilkinson, Jane Kitani, Angels Amore,
Phyllis Lake, Cicero School of Languages and Southwark College.
Special thanks are due to Martyn Ellis and Jan Boldt for their
valuable comments.

D1477554